**CHARTWELL BOOKS, INC.**
A Division of
**BOOK SALES, INC.**
110 Enterprise Avenue
Secaucus, New Jersey 07094

© Ward Lock Limited 1979

First published in Great Britain in 1979
by Ward Lock Limited, London, a Pentos Company.

Reprinted 1980

Printed and bound in Hong Kong
by Leefung-Asco Printers Ltd.

ISBN 0-89009-287-7
Library of Congress No. 79-52752

# Best Loved
# CARS
## OF THE WORLD

**CHARTWELL
BOOKS, INC.**

# Best Loved

# CARS

## OF THE WORLD

## John Plummer

# Contents

# Foreword by
# Lord Montagu
## of Beaulieu

Like most inventions of the last hundred years the motor car is essentially utilitarian, yet it has gathered for itself more romance and nostalgia than any similar invention. Since the second world war its history has attracted the attention of many writers both scholarly and popular, and it might seem that there was little new that could be said on the subject. However with this beautiful book I feel that John Plummer and his publishers have produced a work which is fresh in its approach, authoritative and easy to read, and very attractive to look at. I am personally familiar with many of the cars as they come from The National Motor Museum, and yet the excellent photographs, especially of details, shed a new light on them.

For older readers who remember seeing and driving these fine cars, and the younger generation who want to capture the atmosphere of a past age, I can thoroughly recommend this book.

*Montagu of Beaulieu*

**Lord Montagu of Beaulieu seated at the wheel of an 1899 Daimler.**

# Introduction

The reasons for which the motor car and motoring have so strong an appeal for so many people are numerous and varied. There is the joy of movement and speed, springing from the same basic kinesthetic instinct as dancing and running, gymnastics, sailing or flying. There is satisfaction in the exercise and control of a powerful machine. There is the immense practical import of an adaptable, convenient, readily available means of transport, something which has a bearing on the pattern of all our lives. There is the enormous widening of horizons a car offers, the opportunity for freedom of travel to explore, to visit other people and other events, extending and enriching the individual's experience of the world around him. Then there is the fascination of the car itself. For all machines are fascinating to some degree. The interrelation of components, the ingenuity of the solution to a given problem, the autonomy breathed into a working device by its inventor, all intrigue the curiosity. And the motor car is as complex a machine as many of us ever encounter. The many requirements to which a car designer attempts to conform are often conflicting and sometimes directly contrary, so that he is always engaged in a process of compromise, a delicate balancing act. Within the limits of available techniques, he is endlessly weighing against each other considerations of strength, weight, economy, ease of production, and the accommodation of the human frame. To these are nowadays added safety, comfort, quietness, roadholding, durability, aerodynamics, and a host of other factors. Seldom is he free of fashion, market forces, and the dictates of legislation. That he can balance all these so well, sometimes with such aesthetic as well as practical success, creating a thing of beauty as well as utility, is a fascinating demonstration of man's adaptability, inventiveness, and persistence. Craftsmanship, the basic human activity of making things, lies at the root of it all, even when transmuted through the complexities of modern mass-production. And to look at the craftsmanship of other countries and other times, even of one's own country and time, has not only its own interest but also reveals aspects of the people and of their culture. So the story of the motor car forms one thread in the tapestry of history. To select, then, from so diverse a field just thirty-six or so examples is inevitably to some extent arbitrary. There are cars which represent an important milestone in technical development, and others which become socially significant because of large-scale production although of no great engineering merit. There are cars which exemplify the work of outstanding individuals, and others which reflect a period. Particular cars are marked out by events in which they took part, or by a large access of that character which man-made objects somehow derive from their creators. The selection which follows reflects little a of the variety, color, beauty, and human skill which form part of the motoring scene.

**Above:** the Gothic arch radiator shape identifies this 1908 tourer as a product of the Adams Manufacturing Company Ltd of Bedford, England, who made cars between 1905 and the outbreak of the first world war. Their early designs came from Hewitt of New York, and the American influence showed in the use of a pedal-controlled epicyclic gearbox.

# 1 AMERICA

In the early history of the automobile, many American manufacturers were quick to establish and conform to conventional patterns of engineering, so cars from most of the bigger companies soon came to share basic concepts without much variation. The same general approach led to the adoption of mass-production techniques earlier in America than in Europe. But some firms stood aside from this movement towards consensus, choosing to abide by their own individual decisions. One such was the Franklin company, whose cars remained virtually alone in having air rather than water cooled engines from 1901 to 1934. Shown here is a 1904 model, with a transversely mounted four-cylinder engine hidden under its diminutive hood.

# 1903 Cadillac

Today, the name Cadillac is a synonym of affluence, recognized all over the world as the transport of tycoons and oil sheikhs, familiar in newsreel scenes of arriving heads of state. At one time firms like Hispano-Suiza, Isotta-Fraschini, Horch, Napier, Duesenberg, Packard, and many more vied for prestige in the field of conspicuous luxury at any price. But one by one these grand names faded from the scene, and in recent years Cadillac has risen to a pre-eminence with few rivals. How remote, then, seem the beginnings of Cadillac, the 1903 model shown here. Henry M. Leland was a partner in a general engineering firm whose work included making engines for Oldsmobile. The success of this venture prompted Leland to devise his own car, the Cadillac. Good workmanship made it durable and reliable, and it was cheaper than the contemporary Ford. A reputation began to be established. Cadillac was early in developing standardized production. In 1908, F.S. Bennett, Cadillac's English importer, arranged a demonstration of this. Three single cylinder cars were dismantled and all the parts mixed together. From the assorted components three cars were then reassembled and their reliability proved by a 500 mile run on the Brooklands circuit. For this feat the RAC awarded Cadillac the Dewar Trophy, reserved for outstanding technical achievements.

## The early American automobile

The Cadillac model A, current from 1903 to 1908, is a good example of early car production in the USA. Here, and in the similar designs from firms like Ford and Oldsmobile, a distinctive American style, simple and rugged, had already begun to emerge. A single cylinder engine is mounted amidships with the cylinder horizontal and the crankshaft running across the car. The use of an epicyclic gearbox, with gearing of the sun-and-planet type, was widespread among early American cars, though rare in Europe. A low-revving engine and no great concern for performance made two ratios sufficient, and all the problems of missed changes were eliminated. Chain drive to the centre of the rear axle transmits power to the wheels.

**Above: front end of a 'gas buggy'. A long tube, with fins to increase heat dissipation, forms the simplest kind of radiator. Fashion compelled Cadillac to fit a dummy hood later in the model's life.**

## Specification

**Engine:** Single cylinder, horizontal. Bore 127mm (5in), stroke 127mm (5in), displacement 1609cc (98 cu in). Inlet over exhaust valve. Magneto and trembler coil ignition.

**Transmission:** Two-speed epicyclic gearbox (pedal engages low gear, lever selects high), chain final drive, live axle.

**Brakes:** Single contracting band brake operates on differential.

**Suspension:** Semi-elliptic leaf springs front and rear.

**Maximum speed:** 30 to 40mph (50 to 65km/h).

**Body:** Four-seater tonneau.

Above: it is perhaps difficult to recapture fully the sense of excitement which must have been aroused in the pioneer motorist venturing forth on a machine like this in the first few years of the automobile's history. But though a self-propelled vehicle might be a novelty, the body it carried came straight from the existing tradition of coachbuilding. Like the small horse-drawn buggy to which it is still closely related, the Cadillac provides its passengers with almost no protection against the weather — simplicity and light weight were more important considerations. Oil lamps come from the horse-drawn era too. A basic chassis with two straight sidemembers rides high on leaf springs front and rear, with the engine underneath in the middle. The axles carry wooden-spoked wheels.

Right: the tonneau bodywork has a single central door for access to the rear compartment, just like a governess cart. Visible in this view is the chain drive to a simple differential unit on the rear axle. A band brake fitted round the differential provides the only means of slowing the car. The rear axle is stiffened by a bracing rod underneath.

# 1914 Ford model T

The Ford model T, the 'Tin Lizzie', the first truly mass-produced motor car and until recently the most numerous model ever, must have introduced more people to motoring than anything else on wheels. For this is no mere automobile. It is a phenomenon, a legend, a chapter of folklore, a piece of social history. More than fifteen million model Ts were made at factories in the USA, Canada, and Britain between October 1908 and May 1927. The car was used for every conceivable function a motor vehicle could fulfill. It was seen on every street and every farm at home, it took explorers and prospectors through new territories abroad, it served as a truck and as a racing car, it played a role in the comedy of early films. It became a household word and a part of the scenery, as well as a character in popular mythology, in a way that no car before had. Cheap enough to be widely available, rugged and versatile enough for both private and commercial use in town and country, the T was an integral part of life, particularly in America, something on which people relied as a matter of routine for business and pleasure. In this way it set the precedent for the position occupied by the motor car today: many cars followed it but no single model replaced it.

---

**Specification**

**Engine:** Four cylinders, in line. Bore 101.6mm (4in), stroke 76.2mm (3in), displacement 2472cc (151cu in). Horizontal overhead valves. Coil and HT magneto dual ignition. Maker's hp, 20. RAC hp, 26.

**Transmission:** Epicyclic two-speed gearbox, pedal controlled gearchange, propeller shaft enclosed in torque tube, live axle.

**Brakes:** Footbrake operates contracting band on transmission. Handbrake, for parking, on rear wheels.

**Suspension:** Transverse leaf spring front and rear.

**Wheelbase:** 2540 mm (8 ft 4 in).

**Maximum speed:** 45 mph (72 km/h).

**Body:** Five-seater tourer.

---

### Henry's Tin Lizzie

In the very early years, motor cars tended to be either the expensive pastime of the wealthy, or so feebly underpowered and unreliable as to be of little practical value. Henry Ford's aim was to make a sound, useful automobile cheaply enough to sell in large numbers to ordinary people. With the model T, he succeeded beyond all expectation, and as sales rose he was able to compound the success, and increase the manufacturing capacity of the company.

From an engineering standpoint, the design was not without its weaknesses. But its simplicity and the use of good quality materials enabled it to stand up to hard work, abuse and neglect with amazing fortitude. Lizzie could never have achieved what she did if she had been unreliable. Wire-spoked wheels replaced the wooden ones and such refinements as electric lighting were added, but basically the design did not alter in nineteen years.

Gear changing, the bane of the early motorist, was rendered foolproof by the model T's ingenious gearbox. The lefthand pedal selected low speed when right down, high when right up, with neutral in between. The centre pedal selected reverse (and served as an emergency brake) while the righthand pedal applied a brake on the transmission for normal use. A lever applied the parking brake on the rear wheels and also latched the changespeed pedal in the neutral position. Levers below the steering wheel controlled throttle opening and ignition advance. On the early models a crank handle had to be used to start the engine, but later cars had a starter.

Below: The 1914 model T shown here has five-seater tourer bodywork, one of the most popular forms. For many years, black was the only color available from the factory. Other body styles manufactured during Lizzie's nineteen year run included a phaeton, a two-seater runabout, a doctor's coupé and a 'Fordor' sedan. There was also a one ton truck version, and some people constructed their own bodywork, too. Plenty of ground clearance made Lizzie ideal for rural use.

Right: Lizzie had a brass radiator until 1916, a black painted or sometimes nickel-plated one of less angular shape thereafter, one of the few changes of design in the car's history. Stiff gradients would set the radiator boiling merrily, but model T owners came to accept this as part of the car's indelible and endearing personality. Quite often, steep hills had to be tackled in reverse gear, sometimes because the gravity fuel feed failed, sometimes because the low gear band slipped.

# 1920 Stanley Steamer

The one serious rival to the gasoline (petrol) engine, and its near relative the diesel, as the means of propelling a motor vehicle has been steam power. Long before the practical internal combustion engine emerged, steam carriages were on the roads of Britain in the 1820s and 1830s, though circumstances conspired to make them a false dawn in the history of mechanical road transport. Fifty or sixty years later, in the very early days of motor cars, steam and gasoline looked equally promising, pioneers like the Comte de Dion experimented with both. But in Europe gasoline soon established its supremacy. In America, though, the battle was less decisively won, and the steamer continued to have its adherents for many years. Longest running of all was the Stanley. The twin brothers, F.E. and F.O. Stanley, born in 1849, had a passion for inventing and making things. F.O. Stanley was particularly proud of the violins he made himself. And they were good businessmen, too. Among their inventions was a dry plate photographic process which they sold to Eastman Kodak for a considerable sum. Convinced that they could do better than the early cars they had seen, they built their first steamer in Newton, Massachusetts, in 1897. Its success encouraged the Locomobile company to buy the manufacturing rights, and by 1899 production had reached 200 cars a year. When Locomobile got into difficulties, the Stanleys bought back the rights at a bargain price, and in 1902 launched a redesigned, much improved steamer, leaving Locomobile to make gasoline cars. The Stanley remained in production without major change until 1925, though the brothers retired in 1917.

**Above: the fire chariot of the sun god is the classical device on the Stanley's badge. The radiator, though identical in construction to that of a gasoline engined car, serves in this case as a condenser, recycling water to the boiler and extending the range between fillings.**

## Specification

**Boiler:** Front mounted, cylindrical, fire-tube type with superheater. Diameter 584 or 660mm (23 or 26in) according to model.

**Engine:** Two cylinder, double acting, mounted horizontally. Bore 102mm (4in), stroke 127mm (5in), slide valves operated by Stephenson's link motion.

**Transmission:** Spur gear drive to differential ring gear, ratio 1.5:1.

**Brakes:** Drum brakes on rear wheels.

**Suspension:** Leaf springs, semi-elliptic front, fully elliptic rear.

**Wheelbase:** 3300mm (10ft 10in).

**Cruising speed:** 45mph (72km/h).

**Body:** Two-seater roadster.

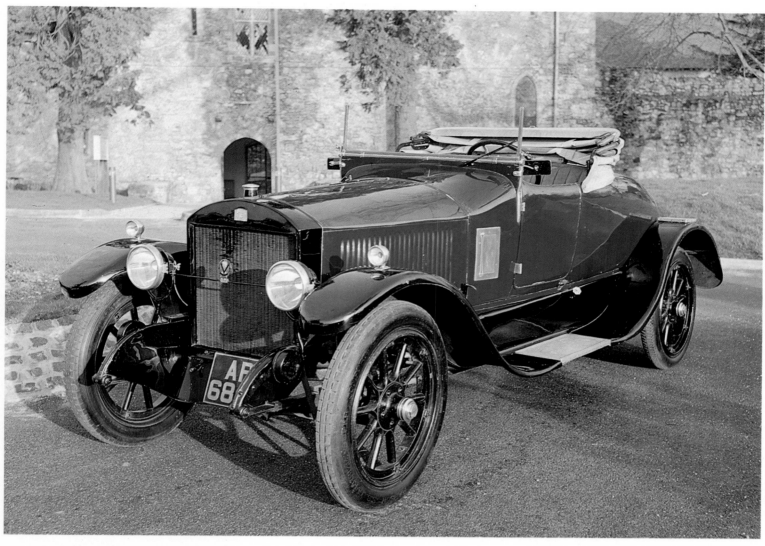

Below: opening the hood (bonnet) reveals not the engine, which is underneath the rear of the car, but the cylindrical casing of the boiler and its attendant plumbing. Beside the boiler is the long horizontal expansion tube and valve of the 'feed water automatic' which controls the water supply.

Above: conventional appearance of this Stanley 735-A, like any two-seater roadster of 1920, belies its unconventional power plant. Stanley publicity material was at pains to point out that it was set apart from 'internal explosive' cars only by the advantages conferred by the steam engine, including

smooth power and simplicity of control. Valance panels between running boards and body conceal the horizontal engine ahead of the rear axle. The body has a rumble (dickey) seat in the tail. Artillery wheels are not easily detachable but carry demountable rims to facilitate tire changing.

## The Steam Car

Simplicity was originally the major attraction of the steam car. Unlike an internal combustion engine (gasoline or diesel) a steam engine can generate a large torque at low speeds, even at a standstill — it is extremely flexible. This means that it can start a vehicle from rest and run right through its speed range with no need for a clutch or for changing gears. It is smooth and quiet, which early gasoline engines were definitely not, and its boiler can be fired with a wide variety of fuels. Power is available in plenty: in 1906 a special Stanley racer raised the land speed record to 121 mph.

Powerful, quiet, gearless and with few moving parts, the steamer yet had one major snag, the time taken to raise steam before starting off. Eight or ten minutes were required for the first start of the day with a Stanley. And a steamer needed perhaps more understanding from its driver: it was less resistant to maltreatment than, say, a model T. So that as the gasoline car improved, the steamer fell behind, its advantages reduced and its

shortcomings highlighted. The introduction of the electric self-starter by Cadillac in 1912 was a major blow. The snags could be overcome, as Abner Doble proved with his superb 1923 steamer which could start from cold in under 90 seconds. But the result was a very complicated motor car which could never compete in price with its opposition.

What the Stanley achieved, it did by staying simple. While other steam car builders, for example, adopted the water-tube or 'flash' boiler in order to raise steam quickly, Stanley stuck to a simple, cylindrical fire-tube boiler. The twin cylinder engine was mounted horizontally, in unit with the rear axle, the differential of which it drove through a single gear. After 1915, a radiator at the front of the car condensed steam exhausted by the engine so that the water was recycled and the range on a filling extended from 50 to over 300 miles. The rest of the car followed conventional contemporary practice. Owners spoke highly of its quietness, good acceleration and reliability.

# 1929 Packard 640

Packard is one of the great names in the history of the American automobile. Though not without rivals — people talked of the 'three Ps' of quality car manufacture, Packard, Peerless, and Pierce-Arrow — the Packard became, perhaps, the best known and most successful of the more expensive cars in America in the twenties. In the quest for refinement and smoothness, first six then twelve-cylinder cars were built. In 1923 came the first eight-cylinder design, and this 'straight-eight' achieved great success, helping Packard to sell 50,000 cars in 1928. It was a connoisseur's car, built to the highest standards of finish and luxury, with a beautifully balanced engine, gear ratios which exactly matched the engine's characteristics, and positive steering. The impressive 1929 model 640 shown here, once the property of the Sultan of Oman, illustrates well what kind of car the Packard was. In shape it is restrained, almost austere, with the simple, classical lines of the vintage tourer, conceived within a well-established style. Yet in other ways, in the use of plated fittings, cellulose paintwork, disc wheels, whitewall tires, it acknowledges the mass-production era and looks forward to much more ornate and showy styles to come.

**Specification**

**Engine:** Eight cylinders, in line. Bore 85.7mm (3.475in), stroke 127mm (5in), displacement 5866cc (358cu in). Side valves, L head. Coil ignition. Power output 106bhp.

**Transmission:** Three-speed gearbox, propeller shaft, live axle.

**Brakes:** Footbrake operates on all four wheels.

**Suspension:** Semi-elliptic leaf springs front and rear.

**Maximum speed:** 65 to 70mph (104 to 112km/h).

**Body:** Four-door tourer.

## Eights and twelves

The brothers J.W. and W.D. Packard built their first car in 1898. It was a typical single-cylinder early American gas buggy, but distinguished by having three forward gears, instead of two. The firm quickly progressed to larger, more refined machinery, and began the quest for a smooth, quiet-running engine. In 1915 Cadillac announced an eight-cylinder car, heralded as the 'most cylindered American automobile'. Partly in answer to this Packard introduced the 'Twin-Six', with a V12 engine of just under 7 litres. It provided an unprecedented level of power, flexibility and freedom from vibration, and began a fashion for twelve-cylinder cars. In 1919 Ralph de Palma drove a 'Twin-Six' at almost 150mph at Daytona. But the V12 was complicated and costly to manufacture, and the straight-eight of 1923 provided a good compromise, less expensive but still very smooth.

**Above: opulence and luxury on a grand scale, late twenties style. Though retaining the simple basic shape of a vintage tourer, this Packard exudes conspicuous affluence and expensive**

Right: all set for a rich owner's fair weather motoring. The separate windshield for rear seat passengers is mounted behind the rear doors, emphasising the length of the car. Quality is evident in every detail. The mounting of the foremost pair of lamps includes a linkage which turns them as the front wheels are steered so that the beams are guided in the intended direction of travel. Gaiters enclose the suspension springs to keep grease in and dirt out. The Packard Eight is recognized as one of the best American cars of the period, the attention to outward finish being backed up by sound engineering. The result was a car for the connoisseur.

quality. A large trunk provides luggage capacity at the rear. Its carrier is mounted on the chassis sidemembers which emerge unashamedly from beneath the body: disc wheels and bright paintwork point the way forward, but at this date the development of the automobile had not yet reached the stage where all the mechanical components and chassis were completely concealed in a bodyshell styled as much for appearance as for function. In the vintage manner, the body, though spacious, still only houses the passengers; luggage, spare wheels and lamps are added outside.

# 1935 Auburn Speedster

A feature of the American motoring scene which developed through the twenties and thirties was a breed of dramatic, luxurious sports cars. Automobiles like the Stutz Black Hawk, Duesenberg, Kissel and Du Pont added charisma to the world of fashionable film stars, financiers, and politicians, forming part of the atmosphere of opulence, excitement and fame surrounding them. The body designers created impressive appearance and the engineers backed it up with extravagant power and performance. One competitor in this field was the Auburn. Though dating back to 1900, the Auburn company really began to make its mark after 1924, under the direction of E.L. Cord, a kind of impressario of unforgettable automobiles. A series of models with eight-cylinder engines was initiated in 1925 and improved through the succeeding years. The 1935 851 Speedster, shown here, was the culmination of this line of development. The body design by Gordon Buehrig, with its high waisted, squat windshield look, has all the evocative manner of the period and uses it to express power and speed in every line. And the supercharged engine ensures that it is not merely a gesture.

## Supercharged Speedster

Beneath its flamboyant exterior, the 851 Speedster is a ruggedly built machine, basically conventional in layout. Auburn engineers appreciated the need for a rigid chassis frame (unlike some of their contemporaries) and specified unusually deep sidemembers with an X-shape central brace as well as the front and rear crossmembers. Conventional leaf springs provide the suspension, controlled by hydraulic shock absorbers. Hydraulic brakes at front and rear have larger drums than was usual at the period. The rear axle incorporates a Columbia two-speed final drive unit, operated from the cockpit through a vacuum servo, enabling the appropriate ratio to be selected to suit load, speed, and road conditions, and providing a choice between low speed acceleration and relaxed, effortless high speed cruising.

The side valve straight-eight engine was supplied by Lycoming, a firm which became a Cord subsidiary. The quality of everything that went into an Auburn was carefully checked, and the engines were run in the test room for up to fourteen hours before installation. The engine has an iron cylinder block, an aluminum cylinder head, and a five-bearing crankshaft fitted with a Lanchester vibration damper. Unsupercharged, it produced 115bhp. With the addition of a Schwitzer-Cummins centrifugal supercharger which runs at six times crankshaft speed (24000rpm at the engine's maximum speed of 4000rpm), power is boosted by a further 35bhp to provide impressive performance.

### Specification

**Lycoming engine:** Eight cylinders, in line. Bore 77.8mm (3.06in), stroke 120.6mm (4.75in), displacement 4587cc (280cu in). Side valve, aluminum L head. Five bearing crankshaft. Centrifugal supercharger. Coil ignition. Power output 150bhp at 4000rpm.

**Transmission:** Three-speed gearbox, propeller shaft, live axle. Two-speed final drive, high ratio 3.47:1, low ratio 5.0:1.

**Brakes:** Pedal operates hydraulic brakes on all four wheels, handbrake operates rear brakes only. Drum diameter 305mm (12in).

**Suspension:** Semi-elliptic leaf springs front and rear, beam axles. Hydraulic shock absorbers. Tire size 6.50 x 16.

**Wheelbase:** 3226mm (10ft 7in).

**Weight:** 1780kg (3920lb).

**Maximum speed:** 100mph (160km/h).

**Body:** Two-seater sports.

**Below: Auburn 851 Supercharged Speedster.** The long wheelbase chassis, typical of this kind of car, gave the body designer maximum freedom to exercise his art in the extrovert idiom of the day. Starting with the high-sided, long-tailed Speedster form already evolved by designers like Sakhnoffsky, Gordon Buehrig blended in the more rounded forms that had begun to appear in the thirties. The result is a form at once massive and suggestive of speed. The deeply skirted wings (fenders) which are a distinctive feature of this car are perhaps a hint of what was to come with the Cord 810 from the same stylist. A flush-fitting panel behind the seats conceals the top when not in use.

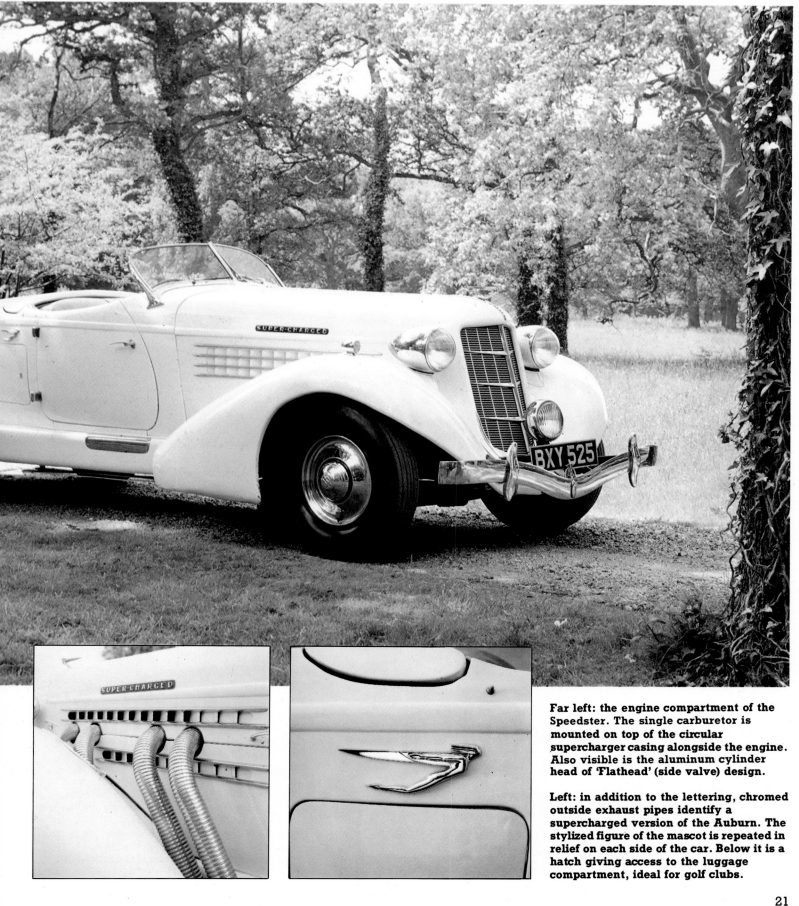

**Far left: the engine compartment of the Speedster.** The single carburetor is mounted on top of the circular supercharger casing alongside the engine. Also visible is the aluminum cylinder head of 'Flathead' (side valve) design.

**Left: in addition to the lettering, chromed outside exhaust pipes identify a supercharged version of the Auburn.** The stylized figure of the mascot is repeated in relief on each side of the car. Below it is a hatch giving access to the luggage compartment, ideal for golf clubs.

21

# 1935 Chrysler Airflow

Commercially, it was one of the biggest failures produced by a major manufacturer. Probably few people can say they really like its looks. Technically, however, it represents an important milestone. For the Chrysler Airflow was the first mass-produced attempt to apply the principles of aerodynamics to a motor car. With the growth of the aircraft industry and a widespread desire for modernity, the thirties produced a good deal of spurious 'streamline' styling, with no scientific basis, on all kinds of vehicles. But Chrysler's efforts were based on serious research, and the Airflow was significantly more 'slippery', less impeded by the drag of its own progress through the air, than other typical contemporary designs. The public was unready for such advances, but it was a brave attempt and paved the way for later progress.

**Milestone of technical advance**

The Chrysler company had already shown itself to be technically advanced, adopting through the early thirties a series of small but important innovations such as flexible engine mountings, an automatic clutch, synchromesh in the gearbox, and an overdrive actuated by the throttle pedal. So it was natural that it should become involved with the developing science of aerodynamics.

Much of the basic work had been done in the twenties. In particular, Paul Jaray, born in Vienna, at one time chief-designer at the Zeppelin airship works, had shown that careful attention to the body shape could dramatically reduce air drag so that a car went faster and accelerated more rapidly on the same power and used less fuel — almost a third less in some cases. Attendant benefits of less noise, greater stability and better ventilation could result as well. In 1928, Chrysler commissioned Jaray, then working as a consulant in Switzerland, to design a prototype. Carrying on his work by road testing full size cars and using models in a wind tunnel, Chrysler engineers Carl Breer and James Zeder evolved the Airflow which first appeared in 1934. It was a compromise between the best that could be achieved aerodynamically and the practicalities of carrying six passengers, but at 85mph it generated 20 per cent less drag than a contemporary conventional sedan.

**Left: frontal aspects of the Airflow. Narrow wings (fenders) flank a body of great width than was usual. Cars imported to Britain, like this righthand drive example, were named after London's two developing airports, Heston (for six cylinder models) and Croydon (for eight cylinder models), emphasising the Airflow's appeal to the contemporary fashion for ultra-modernity. The blossoming civil aviation industry provided a new vocabulary for automobile sales staff to plunder as the streamline style spread.**

Below: headlamps are faired in to the body (in contrast to the added auxiliary lamps on this example). The basic form may have come from scientific research, but the details of its execution and the added ornamentation bear witness to the 'art deco' fashion of the period.

Above: the first Airflows had a wide, plated radiator grille curving backwards on the same line as the body each side. Worried by the unfavorable public reaction to the car, Chrysler hastily added the more protruding dummy hood (bonnet) and grille seen on this

1935 model. It helped the Airflow to survive until 1937, although a more normal-looking 'Airstream' series was introduced in 1935 to maintain sales. Aerodynamically inspired features of the design include spats covering the rear wheel arches and a 'fastback' shape.

## Specification

**Engine:** Eight cylinders, in line. Displacement 5301cc (323cu in). Side valves, L head. Coil ignition.

**Transmission:** Three-speed gearbox with helical-cut gears and synchromesh. Overdrive on second and top gears, operated by accelerator. Free wheel operative with overdrive engaged.

**Brakes:** Drum brakes on all four

wheels, handbrake operates rear brakes.

**Suspension:** Semi-elliptic leaf springs front and rear.

**Wheelbase:** 3251mm (10ft 8in).

**Body:** Four-door six-seater sedan.

# 1936 Ford V8 'Woody'

Quite early in the history of the automobile, as soon as it progressed beyond mere novelty and became a useful machine, owners began to modify the bodywork to suit their own particular needs. A small farmer might not be able to afford a new truck, for example, but he could buy a second hand Ford model T and construct his own truck body on the chassis. If he kept window openings, whether glazed or not, and if it was still occasionally used to carry people as well as hay, it might evolve into a station wagon or estate car. In its rougher forms, it could look a bit like an accident involving an old car and somebody's chicken shed. But it did not have to be like that, and as the usefulness and popularity of the dual-purpose vehicle became clear, the car manufacturers themselves took up the idea. The woodwork, originally the only material available to the amateur coachbuilder or small firm, turned into a smartly varnished feature rather than a necessity, and the 'Woody' became an accepted style. While the wood framing retained its structural purpose, all was well (if not always rot-proof), even after wood panelling gave way to metal. Unfortunately, the style persisted after all vestiges of its rationale had gone, leading to the absurdities of pressed steel bodies carefully shaped and painted to look like wood, and, latterly, glued-on 'wood-grain' plastic.

## The Ford V8

The very success of the model T, as the years passed, provided Ford with a thorny problem: what to do next, how to replace a legend that has finally outrun its time? The answer, the model A, appeared after a six months' factory shut-down in 1927, and was a conventional four-cylinder design. The next development followed in 1932 with the introduction of the V8. Other American manufacturers had produced V8 engines, beginning with Cadillac in 1915, but not in the numbers Ford intended, for once production was well established it became the firm's only model. Production reached one million in 1935.

The V8 kept the transverse leaf spring suspension of both its predecessors, the T and the A, and at first body styles were similar to the A. But a new, more streamlined look soon appeared, the front end of which is retained in the version illustrated here. The side valve ('flathead') V8 engine was the heart of the design, powerful yet uncomplicated, a unit which was to stay in production until 1954 and prove successful in many applications.

---

**Specification**

**Engine:** Eight cylinders in V. Bore 77.8mm (3.06in), stroke 95mm (3.75in), displacement 3614cc (221cu in). Side valves, L heads. Coil ignition. Power output 70bhp.

**Transmission:** Three-speed gearbox, propeller shaft enclosed in torque tube, live axle.

**Brakes:** Mechanically operated drum brakes front and rear.

**Suspension:** Transverse leaf springs front and rear.

**Wheelbase:** 2692mm (8ft 10in).

**Body:** 'Woody' estate car.

Above: the marriage of two entirely different methods of construction characterises the 'Woody'. The front end has pressed steel panels, exactly the same, in this case, as a contemporary Ford V8 sedan. The remainder of the body is framed and panelled in wood, with a square cut shape which suits both the material and the vehicle's utility purpose. Here the wood is still structural, though on post-war examples it was sometimes merely decoration on an all-steel body. Carefully fitted joints, beaded edges to the framing, and the elegant curve of the cantrails above the side windows show how the traditional style of the craftsman woodworker survived in the 'Woody', to be placed in strange counterpoint with the up-to-the-minute streamline design of the front grille and sidelamps.

Far left: running boards and rear wings (fenders) are retained from the sedan, as is the spare wheel cover. A drop-down tailgate, with, in this case, a canvas screen above, gives the vehicle its dual-purpose character, enabling large loads to be carried.

Left: above the badge is a V8 emblem. Ford's adoption of the V8 as their only American model until 1941 made it a familiar sight.

# 1937 Cord Beverly

Under three different banners, the cars of Errett Lobban Cord brought a touch of drama and excitement to an otherwise fairly dreary and conventional phase in American automobile history. In 1924, he acquired and revitalised the Auburn company. In 1926, he added the opulent Duesenberg to his empire. But the most striking of the trio came last and was the only one to bear his name. Flamboyant styling, luxury, and prodigious performance, all three had: to these qualities the Cord added technical originality. When racing car builder Harry Miller began to make his mark at American track races like Indianapolis with a front wheel drive design, E.L. Cord bought the patent rights for use in road cars. The first result was the Cord L29, with body design still in the traditional mode, though the use of front wheel drive allowed a longer and lower look than even the Duesenberg. But 1929 was not a propitious year to launch such an exotic and expensive creation, and the Depression had brought production to a halt by 1932. For its reappearance in 1935, the Cord took another step forward. Gordon Buehrig, stylist of the Auburn speedster, clothed the new 810 in a body as revolutionary as its mechanical specification. Owing more, perhaps, to the aircraft industry than to contemporary automobile design, it was streamlined, dramatic, and in a futuristic class of its own. The supercharged 812 version followed in 1936, giving 100 mph performance and adding formidable acceleration to the Cord's impressive appearance and advanced specification.

## E. L. Cord's last attempt

The Cord L29 had a straight-eight engine, like the Auburn's and Miller-inspired de Dion beam axle front suspension. For the new car these were replaced by a more compact V8 power unit and a new independent front suspension with each wheel carried on a trailing arm. A further innovation was a body and chassis integrated into a unitary structure.

From the engine the drive was taken forwards to a four-speed gearbox which had an electro-vacuum servo change mechanism. Gears were selected in advance by a finger tip lever in a miniature gate on the steering column, the changes being made by depressing the clutch pedal.

Perhaps insufficient time was allowed to perfect all these new features at once. Possibly American buyers were more conservative about mechanical things than about body styling. Perhaps the price was just too high. And the economic climate did not help. Whatever the reason, the Cord failed to survive 1937. But it had been a brave gamble and a glorious swan song, and car design could never be quite the same again.

---

### Specification

**Lycoming engine:** Eight cylinders in V. Bore 88.9 mm (3.5 in), stroke 95.2 mm (3.75 in), displacement 4730 cc (289 cu in). Side valves, L heads. Centrifugal supercharger gear driven from camshaft. Coil ignition. Power output 170 bhp at 4200 rpm.

**Transmission:** Four-speed gearbox with electro-vacuum pre-selector change mechanism, front wheel drive through Rzeppa constant velocity universal joints.

**Brakes:** Hydraulically operated drum brakes on all four wheels.

**Suspension:** Independent front with transverse leaf spring, half-elliptic rear.

**Wheelbase:** 3175 mm (10 ft 5 in)

**Maximum speed:** 100 mph (160 km/h)

**Body:** Four door sedan, integral structure.

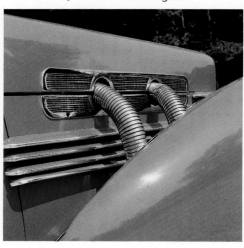

Below: Retractable headlamps are one of the Cord 812's futuristic features.

Above: Buehrig's styling is free of unnecessary ornamentation and startlingly original in its impact.

Left: Chromed outside exhaust pipes distinguish a model 812 fitted with the optional supercharger.

Right: The view other drivers got of a Cord sedan. The streamline style matters more than visibility to the rear

Among the smaller, more specialized British car makers, the AC company is notable for a long and varied history. Production began in 1908 with a lightweight three-wheeler delivery truck, the Autocarrier, from which a two-seater car, the AC Sociable, was derived. In 1954 the Ace sports car appeared, later to be transformed at Carroll Shelby's instigation into the fast and formidable Ford V8 engined Cobra. Between these extremes, in the inter-war years, the company produced a series of light cars of some distinction. This 1921 tourer has an Anzani side-valve engine of 1½ litres. An unconventional feature is the location of the three-speed gearbox, to which a disc transmission brake is attached, in unit with the rear axle.

# 1908 Lanchester 20hp

Among the engineers involved with the motor car in the early days, Frederick Lanchester is an outstanding figure. His clear perception and inventive genius produced highly original and satisfactory solutions to many of the fundamental problems of car design, and his work predated much later developments in many ways. Some of the things he introduced stayed in current use, others were forgotten only to be rediscovered later; for example, Lanchester patented a disc brake in 1903. Basic principles, like the need for soft springs and a rigid chassis for an effective suspension system, he grasped in a way that none of his contemporaries seem to have done. His first prototype car was made in 1895, and Lanchester and his two brothers formed a company in 1899. Other cars of the period tended to be a somewhat ill-assorted combination of stationary engine design and horse-drawn carriage practice, with a few parts borrowed from the bicycle manufacturer. Once a reasonably workable formula had emerged from the work of Benz and Daimler in Germany, de Dion and Panhard in France, many builders tended to imitate rather than initiate. But the Lanchester was designed from the start as a motor car, a complete entity with no borrowed ideas, and it was remarkably efficient and reliable.

## Lanchester's advanced design

Among the unconventional features which made the early Lanchesters smooth riding, controllable cars were a strong, light unit construction chassis and lower body section, and long cantilever springs in conjunction with radius arms to locate the axles. The suspension was arranged to have a natural frequency of rise and fall little different from that of a man walking, and the driving position, too, gave an eye level similar to walking, both calculated to ensure the driver's well-being and comfort, and to enable him to judge speed and distance naturally and accurately. Tiller steering gave the driver quick, effortless control.

These features were retained on the 1908 20hp model shown here, but the centrally mounted flat-twin engine of the earlier cars was replaced by an upright four-cylinder engine compact enough to fit between the front seats, increasing the available rear seat legroom.

**Above:** the tubular front axle is set well out in front on long springs. There is no hood behind the radiator as the engine is between the front seats.

**Left:** Lanchester designed the 20hp chassis to accept a variety of body styles: this single landaulette provides covered accommodation only for rear seat passengers, but other types had full-length roofs. The long wheelbase enables the car to be slung comfortably between the axles. The steering tiller enters the cockpit from the side. With no steering wheel in the way a sloping apron is fitted to protect occupants of the front seats: it can be tilted up for access.

### Specification

**Engine:** Four cylinders, in line. Bore 101.6mm (4in), stroke 76.2mm (3in), displacement 2472cc (151cu in). Horizontal overhead valves. Coil and HT magneto dual ignition. Maker's hp, 20. RAC hp, 26.

**Transmission:** Three-speed epicyclic gearbox with preselector control of first and second gear. Propeller shaft, worm final drive, live axle.

**Brakes:** Footbrake operates drums on rear wheels, handbrake operates disc on transmission.

**Suspension:** Long cantilever springs front and rear, with radius arms. Wire wheels. Tiller steering.

**Wheelbase:** 3175mm (10ft 5in).

**Body:** Single landaulette.

# 1913 Rolls-Royce Alpine Eagle

The best car in the world: that was the uncompromising claim made for the Rolls-Royce in the Edwardian years. Right from the outset, its makers sought perfection, confident in the knowledge that customers would always be found willing to pay for it. Henry Royce was a meticulous engineer engaged in manufacturing electric cranes. Dissatisfied with the finish and workmanship of the cars he could buy in 1903, he built one to his own exacting standards. The Honourable Charles Rolls, aristocratic motoring enthusiast and salesman, and his partner Claude Johnson, first secretary of the Automobile Club and organiser of early motoring competitions, were in business selling Panhard et Levassor and Minerva cars imported from France and Belgium. So impressed were they with the quietness and efficiency of Royce's machine that they agreed, at the end of 1904, to take all the cars his firm produced. The formation of Rolls-Royce Ltd. followed in 1906. The Silver Ghost established the company's reputation, and the Alpine Eagle represents the ultimate development of that model before 1914 and the outbreak of war. 'Best car in the world' is bound to be a spark for controversy rather than an irrefutable fact, but the period could hardly have produced a grander, more opulent, or more refined vehicle to convey its wealthy owner on a Continental progress than the example shown here.

## Silver Ghost and Alpine Eagle

The Silver Ghost appeared in 1906, two years later the formation of the Rolls-Royce partnership: in 1907 it became their only model. Though not very advanced in concept, the craftsmanship and attention to detail which went into its making produced an unprecedented degree of refinement (Vauxhall's Pomeroy acidly called it 'a triumph of workmanship over design') and drivers poured superlatives on its smooth, silent, effortless performance. Well publicised demonstrations, such as a London to Edinburgh run in top gear, enhanced its reputation.

But when James Radley ran his Silver Ghost in the 1912 Austrian Alpine Trial, it was forced to stop and drop two passengers in order to climb the Katschberg, and the image took a severe knock. The answer was the Continental model, with changes that included more power, different gearing, and cantilever rear springs to cope better with rough roads. It dominated the 1913 event, after which it became known as the Alpine Eagle. This version formed the basis for the post-war Silver Ghost, which remained in production until 1924.

**Left: Continental touring in the grand manner was the role envisaged for this noble machine. Impressive at rest, it must have been an awe-inspiring sight at speed. The most stylish, effortless, luxurious form of travel that the Edwardian era could offer — other than having your own train, perhaps — is represented by this kind of motor car, a complement to the country house and the yacht, the nearest thing to a magic carpet in an age when the airplane was still only in its infancy. The long wheelbase allows the body to be slung between the axles, rather than riding above them, for comfort and stability. A separate windshield, folded away in this picture, is available to protect passengers in the rear seats.**

**Above:** The famous 'Silver Lady' Rolls-Royce mascot surmounts a classically simple radiator which sets a tone of restrained grandeur for the whole car. Simple, well-proportioned coachwork matches the achievement of the engineer: there is as yet none of the exaggerated showmanship that was to beset some later attempts at body design in this category. The alloy hood conceals an ample $7\frac{1}{2}$ litre engine, a design that was to remain in production until 1924.

**Far left:** Long cantilever rear springs, an idea learned from Lanchester, ensure a smooth ride over broken and rutted roads. The massive proportions of the chassis sidemember can be appreciated in this view. The wide running boards provide stowage space for the impedimenta of long-distance travel.

**Left:** The handbrake lever remains outside the body, and no door is provided for the driver. Among the nickel-plated fittings are both a serpentine bulb horn and a klaxon to ensure adequate warning of the car's approach. Windshield wipers have yet to appear, and the windshield frame can be adjusted for angle or folded flat.

**Specification**

**Engine:** Six cylinders, in line, in two blocks of three. Bore 114 mm (4.5 in), stroke 121 mm (4.8 in), displacement 7428 cc (453 cu in). Side valve, non-detachable L heads. HT magneto and coil ignition. Makers rating 40/50 hp. Power output approximately 70 bhp.

**Transmission:** Cone clutch, four-speed gearbox, live axle.

**Brakes:** On rear wheels.

**Suspension:** Front, half-elliptic leaf springs. Rear, cantilever leaf springs.

**Wheelbase:** 3645 mm (11 ft 11.5 in)

**Maximum speed:** 85 mph (137 km/h).

**Body:** Four-seater tourer.

# 1914 Vauxhall 'Prince Henry'

Epitome of the elegance and simplicity of Edwardian motor car design at its best, the Vauxhall Prince Henry impresses immediately by the sense which it somehow conveys of harmony and of fitness for its purpose. And this impression does not result from qualities merely skin-deep: for the design, by the distinguished engineer Laurence H. Pomeroy, was quickly recognised as a masterpiece of its day, combining refinement and responsiveness with performance of a kind that had hitherto been largely the prerogative of stark, brutal racing machines. If 75 mph does not seem enormously fast by the standards of today, remember that an average sort of motor car of the period would have been capable of something between 35 and 50 mph, which clearly puts the Vauxhall in a special class. The model is sometimes hailed as the first British sports car, but perhaps Grand Tourer better invokes its qualities. Its name derives from the long-distance trials of reliability and speed organised in Germany at the behest of Prince Henry of Prussia. Considerable prestige attached to these trials, and Vauxhall entered a team of cars in the 1910 event against much larger-engined opposition. Though Austro-Daimlers finished in the first three places, the Vauxhalls attracted much favourable comment for their reliable performance, and the name was adopted for the subsequent production model.

**Above: Pomeroy's 4 litre engine produced 75 bhp at what was then the elevated speed of 2500 rpm. Long stroke design was the order of the day, partly because both taxation and competition rules assessed engine capacity, oddly, by cylinder bore but not piston stroke.**

**Above right: Elegance, simplicity and harmony — the Vauxhall Prince Henry was a beautifully proportioned and balanced design. No part looks clumsy or too heavy.**

**Right: Stylish transport for the Edwardian sporting motorist. Contemporary testers praised the Prince Henry for its controlability and high performance achieved with an engine of relatively modest size. The radiator flutes extending into the hood were a famous Vauxhall motif for many years. But only the Prince Henry had the sharply pointed prow. Weather protection is provided by the superb top (hood) shown erected in this view.**

## Specification

**C type engine:** Four cylinders, in line. Bore 95 mm (3.7 in), stroke 140 mm (5.5 in), displacement 3969 cc (242 cu in). Side valves, L head. HT magneto ignition. Makers rating 25 hp. Power output 75 bhp at 2500 rpm.

**Transmission:** Multi disc clutch, four-speed gearbox, propeller shaft, live axle.

**Brakes:** Footbrake on transmission, handbrake on rear wheels.

**Suspension:** Half-elliptic leaf springs front and rear.

**Maximum speed:** 75 mph (120 km/h).

**Body:** Four-seater tourer.

## Vauxhall's sporting cars

Following early experiments with petrol engines for marine use, the Vauxhall company began car manufacture in the early years of the century. After 1905 and the move to Luton from the original Vauxhall Ironworks site in London, they began to compete in racing, hill climbs, and reliability trials, winning the RAC 2,000 Mile Trial in 1908. Competition served as a spur to development, producing the first 3 litre car to reach 100 mph, at the Brooklands circuit in 1910. This 3 litre engine powered the Prince Henry Trial cars, and was then enlarged to 4 litres for sale to the public in 1913. A special version, further enlarged to 4½ litres for use at the British Shelsley Walsh hill climb, provided the basis for the 30/98 model, which was to become even more celebrated in the twenties than the Prince Henry had been before the first world war.

# 1923 Alvis 12/40

The early twenties saw the emergence onto the British motoring scene of a new kind of sports car. Lighter, cheaper, and with smaller engines than the powerful Bentley or Vauxhall of the period, these machines often had only relatively modest performance, but they were more stylish than the ordinary tourer and found a ready market among the growing ranks of the well-to-do middle class. Firms like Calthorpe, Hillman, Jowett, Singer, and many more, listed such a car alongside the more prosaic models in their range. Simple but effective, they were pleasant and practical vehicles, and well suited to British roads, which tended to be narrow and winding, but smoother and less mountainous than those of Europe. A typical specification included a side valve engine of 1100 or 1500cc. A cone clutch was usual, and more often than not a three-speed gearbox was deemed sufficient, though some of the more expensive examples like Alvis had four-speed units. Synchromesh was still a thing of the future, as were brakes on the front wheels. Electric lamps had arrived, so nocturnal motoring, if still not easy, was no longer a struggle with inefficient oil lamps or troublesome acetylene burners. Elegant two-seater bodies, often panelled in aluminum, usually provided occasional seats for additional passengers in a fold-out rumble at the rear. They might be less dramatic than the Edwardian grand tourers, and unrefined by the standards of today, yet these vehicles show very clearly how far the motor car had progressed in twenty or thirty years since its birth.

## Early days at Alvis

The Alvis was distinguished among the light sports cars of the early twenties by high quality, durability, and better than average performance and handling. Founded in 1919 by T.G. John and G.P.H. de Freville, the Alvis company took the name originally coined by de Freville for a type of aluminum piston he had designed. The first Alvis was the 10/30, with an efficient 1460cc side valve engine. In 1922 the bore size of the engine was enlarged to produce the 12/40, an example of which is illustrated on these pages. Lack of capital threatened Alvis with financial disaster in 1924, but the success of the next model, the 12/50, with an OHV engine designed in 1923 by Captain G.T. Smith-Clarke, saved the day. The 12/50 in Super Sports form was capable of 70mph and had excellent handling. Its reputation was boosted by competition results, including a win in the 1923 Brooklands 200 miles race. By 1928, the total number of Alvis cars manufactured had reached 6000.

**Above: radiator mascots were still very much in vogue and Alvis adopted this charming model of a standing hare for their early cars. The distinctive red triangle badge made its last appearance on the TE21 model, made from 1965 until 1967 when Rover acquired Alvis.**

**Top right: low set headlamps flank the honeycomb radiator, while the sidelamps are mounted on the scuttle by the windshield. The lighting is electric. The front axle has no brakes, and the starting handle is still prominent, though a starter motor is fitted.**

**Specification**

**Engine:** Four cylinders, in line. Bore 68mm (2.7in), stroke 110mm (4.3in), displacement 1598cc (98cu in). Side valves, L head. Magneto ignition. Power output 40bhp.

**Transmission:** Cone clutch, four-speed gearbox, propeller shaft, live axle.

**Brakes:** Mechanically operated drum brakes on rear wheels.

**Suspension:** Semi-elliptic leaf springs front and rear.

**Wheelbase:** 2794mm (9ft 2in).

**Maximum speed:** 60 to 65mph (96 to 104km/h).

**Body:** Two-seater with rumble seat.

Above: simple, well built, and stylish, this 1923 Alvis 12/40 exemplifies the qualities of a kind of light, sporting two-seater which was popular in Britain in the twenties. Two additional passengers can be accommodated in the rumble seat, though it seems unlikely to have been intended for long journeys! Other body styles fitted to this type of chassis included a 'beetle-back' two-seater with no rumble, and four-seater tourers. The twenties spawned an amazing number of car manufacturers, and many of them produced models of this general layout. But many, too, were short lived. Of those that endured, the Alvis was notable for good performance and high quality, reflected in a higher than average price.

# 1923 Austin 7

The Austin Seven is one of those rare cars which has become as much a part of folklore as a piece of engineering. Like the Ford model T, it provided transport for thousands of new motorists — 'The Motor for the Millions' was the slogan which hailed its introduction. For its low price and low running costs — about a penny a mile, the makers claimed — extended the possibility of car ownership far wider than ever before. The owner-driver no longer needed to be wealthy: nor did he need to be an eccentric, car-mad tinkerer, for the Seven was virtually the first really practical small car. And it was very small, less than three metres (nine feet) long, though designed to accommodate two adults and three small children. Its diminutive size and cheeky appearance endeared it to the public, and it became the subject of jokes, cartoons and publicity stunts, as well as appearing on stage in music halls. Intended by its makers as a family car, shopping car, businessman's car, and 'tender for the country house', it was used for a multitude of other purposes as well. It was transformed into sports cars and racing cars, it was driven across country and across continents. It was fitted with a variety of special bodies, including the Swallow made by William Lyons, later the builder of Jaguars. It was made under licence in France (Rosengart), Germany (Dixi, the first BMW car), Japan (Datsun), and America (American Austin, later Bantam). It inspired a devoted band of followers which still exists today, restoring and maintaining those Sevens that survive.

## Specification

**Engine:** Four cylinders, in line. Bore 56mm (2.2in), stroke 76.2mm (3in), displacement 747cc (45.6cu in). Main bearings, ball and roller (front), roller (rear). Side valves, L head. Magneto ignition. RAC rating 7.8hp. Power output 10.5bhp at 2400rpm.

**Transmission:** Single dry plate clutch, three-speed gearbox, propeller shaft, torque tube, live axle.

**Brakes:** Footbrake operates rear drums, handbrake operates front drums.

**Suspension:** Transverse leaf spring, front. Quarter-elliptic leaf springs, rear.

**Wheelbase:** 1905mm (6ft 3in).

**Maximum speed:** 38mph (61km/h).

**Body:** two-door four-seater 'Chummy' tourer.

## The first practical small car

Just before and just after the first world war, the only small, cheap cars available in Britain came from a handful of cyclecar manufacturers. The designs of these machines usually owed more to enthusiasm and optimism than to engineering principles and they were mostly impractical, unreliable, and short-lived. Sir Herbert Austin's aim in producing the Seven was to provide a practical, dependable small car with none of the shortcomings of either the cyclecar or the motorcycle and sidecar combination which was gaining popularity. At the same time he hoped to restore the ailing fortunes of the Austin company, which was suffering badly, as were many others, in the slump which followed the first world war.

That he succeeded in these aims is shown by the fact that the Seven remained in production from 1923 to 1938, by which time something over a quarter of a million had been made. Low price, economy, reliability, and small size were the Seven's virtues, allied to its irresistible charm, and it was of little account to its owners and devotees that it had some shortcomings by the general standards applicable to other cars. It was, for example, not the most directionally stable of vehicles, requiring constant corrections of its wanderings by the driver on anything but a smooth road. Though it had four wheel brakes, they were notoriously feeble. And the clutch was rather 'sudden', with very little pedal travel between in and out. But at least it was good training for the driver: if you could drive a Seven competently, you could probably drive anything. For its character and for conferring the gift of motoring on many previously without it, it will be remembered long after motor cars of merely dull competence are forgotten.

YA7103

**Above:** the Austin Seven in its earliest form is represented by this 1923 'Chummy'. Full of charm and character, it was the first really practical small car to be made in large numbers. Within its diminutive proportions it could accommodate two adults and two or three small children, and the top and side curtains protected them from the weather. Body styles produced for later models included sedans, sports versions, and a delivery van.

**Top left:** ignition advance and retard and fuel mixture controls are provided in the centre of the dished steering wheel. An ammeter is the only instrument on the dashboard.

**Top right:** electric head/side lamps are mounted on the scuttle, fed from the dynamo and battery. The lamps on this example are nickel plated, as were earlier acetylene burners, but black enamel was normal in later years.

**Bottom left:** a water temperature gauge which fitted into the radiator cap was a popular accessory. With no water pump in the thermo-siphon cooling system, the driver had to keep a wary eye on the gauge in hilly country.

**Bottom right:** a spare wheel is carried on the tail. The tiny brake drums and the quarter elliptic springs carrying the rear axle are evident in this view.

# 1924 Morris Cowley

The Cowley was the car with which W.R. Morris introduced mass-production methods to the British motor industry. Morris had opened a bicycle shop in Oxford in 1893, was experimenting with motorcycles by 1902, and launched the Morris Oxford car in 1912. The Cowley followed three years later and remained in production until 1934, although losing its distinctive Bullnose radiator in 1926. The Cowley was one of the best of many cars of its general size and type which were vying for the British market in the mid twenties. By ensuring efficient and cheap production, Morris was able to cut his prices drastically in 1921 and 1922. As a result the Cowley comfortably outsold every other contemporary model, and the Morris company survived the difficult years at the end of that decade when so many smaller car firms went out of business.

**Above: from the rear, the Cowley is very like any other tourer of the period. But it out-sold them all and firmly established itself as the popular family car in Britain.**

**Right: the fondly remembered Bullnose Morris. The nickname seems most likely to have been a corruption of 'bullet nosed', an apt description of the distinctive radiator shape. The post-war**

Oxford was at first simply a slightly better equipped version of the same car, but had a larger engine after 1924. Front brakes were not fitted to Cowleys until 1926, so this 1924 model is without them. A can of gasoline on the running board — 'Pratts Motor Spirit' in this case — was a wise precaution, for filling stations were often few and far between on country roads.

## Best-selling family car

Good all-round design without major faults characterized the Cowley. Morris studied American techniques in his quest for efficiency, and the Cowley was at first fitted with an engine supplied to his specification by the Continental company of Detroit. After 1918 he supervised the manufacture of the same engine in Coventry by the English subsidiary of the French Hotchkiss company. As he prospered, Morris was able to take over such component manufacturers, ensuring continuity of supply and laying the foundations for what was to become the Nuffield Organisation, embracing Morris, Wolseley, MG and Riley.

### Specification

**Engine:** Four cylinders, in line. Bore 69.5mm (2.7in), stroke 102mm (4in), displacement 1548cc (94cu in). Side valves, L head. HT magneto ignition. RAC rating 11.9hp. Power output 26bhp at 2800rpm.

**Transmission:** Dual plate wet clutch, three-speed gearbox, enclosed propeller shaft, live axle.

**Brake:** Footbrake and handbrake on rear wheels, four shoes per drum.

**Suspension:** Half-elliptic leaf springs, front. Three-quarter-elliptic leaf springs, rear.

**Wheelbase:** 2591mm (8ft 6in).

**Maximum speed:** 50mph (80km/h).

**Body:** Four-seater tourer.

# 1925 Rolls-Royce Phantom 1

The twenties were marked by a great upsurge in popular motoring in Britain as models like the Austin Seven and Morris Cowley spread car ownership much more widely than ever before. But at the other end of the scale, the market first established during the Edwardian era for cars of sumptuous luxury and great cost continued to exist. Foremost in the field was still Rolls-Royce, though not without competition from Napier, Daimler (who had Royal patronage to enhance their reputation), the larger Lanchesters, and foreign interlopers such as Hispano-Suiza and, from America, a new source of rivalry, the Packard. Having pursued a one-model policy with the Silver Ghost for many years, Rolls-Royce added a smaller car, the 3.2 litre Twenty, in 1922. When the time finally came for the Ghost to be replaced, with the attendant problems of creating a worthy successor to such a celebrated model, the Phantom was introduced, appearing in 1925. Much of the character of the Ghost was retained, little improvement being required. A new engine provided the power to ensure that performance was in the same class as the best of its rivals. As before, grand bodies of superlative quality were created by coachbuilding firms such as Barker, Hooper, and Park Ward.

**Above: driving compartment of the Phantom. Ignition advance and mixture strength controls protrude from the top of the steering column, along with a governor lever enabling a selected cruising speed to be maintained automatically, uphill or down. The windshield is in three sections, and the two halves of the upper part can be opened independently.**

## The New Phantom

Such had been the success of the Silver Ghost that Rolls-Royce were in no hurry to make unnecessary changes when designing the new car. The chassis of the 'New Phantom', as it was initially called, was very similar to that of its predecessor. It retained the long, cantilever rear springs, arguably a somewhat dated feature by 1925. In combination with wider section, lower pressure tires than were used on the Ghost, they could produce an unpleasant floating motion at the rear of the car under some circumstances. Improved shock absorbers, fitted in 1927, helped, but when the Phantom 2 appeared in 1929 it had semi-elliptic rear springs.

The art of engine design had progressed in a number of directions since the days of the Ghost's creation, and among the engines of rival manufacturers were to be found V12 units, straight-eights, and overhead camshaft six-cylinder types. Rolls-Royce designed, built, and tested prototypes of each of these configurations. They experimented, too, with supercharging as a means of increasing the power output, before rejecting it as noisy, complicated, and uneconomical. But

what finally emerged as the Phantom power unit was none of these. Paying great attention, as usual, to achieving smoothness and quietness as well as ample power, Rolls-Royce chose to retain a six-cylinder layout, like the Ghost, but with pushrod operated overhead valves, an engine not unlike that of the Twenty, though much larger. The cylinders were still in two blocks of three, sharing a single detachable cylinder head. Though not officially disclosed, the power output of this unit was in the region of 100bhp. And every bit of it was needed to produce good acceleration, for the maximum total weight permitted by the makers for a laden Phantom 1 was 2952kg (58cwt).

To cope with that kind of weight and 80mph performance, the Phantom had four wheel brakes operated by an ingenious and effective mechanical servo. The system was adapted from one introduced in 1919 by Hispano-Suiza, to whom Rolls-Royce paid royalties for its use. Power for the system came from a disc clutch continuously driven from the gearbox. Movement of the brake pedal began to apply the rear brakes, and also engaged the servo clutch so that the driver's effort was greatly amplified.

**Above: luggage still goes outside. A trunk proudly emblazoned with the Rolls-Royce monogram rides on a carrier above the 20-gallon fuel tank — necessary to satisfy the 10 to 14mpg thirst owners could expect from the 7.6 litre engine. The size of the wheels helps emphasize the massive proportions of the Phantom.**

**Specification**

**Engine:** Six cylinders, in line, in two blocks of three. Bore 108mm (4.25in), stroke 140mm (5.5in), displacement 7668cc. (468cu in). Pushrod operated overhead valves. Dual ignition by coil and magneto. RAC rating 43.3hp. Power output approximately 100bhp at 2750rpm.

**Transmission:** Single dry plate clutch, four-speed gearbox, propeller shaft, live axle.

**Brakes:** Mechanically operated drum brakes on all four wheels.

**Suspension:** Semi-elliptic leaf springs, front. Quarter-elliptic leaf springs, rear.

**Wheelbase:** 2896mm (9ft 6in).

**Maximum speed:** 90mph (145km/h).

**Body:** Four-door sports sedan.

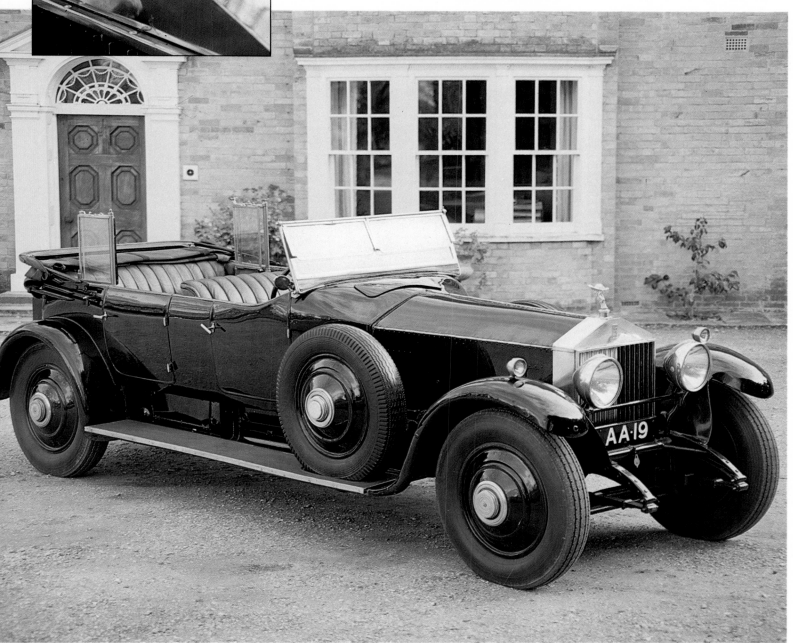

**Top: famous Rolls-Royce emblems. The Phantom retains the classical radiator and mascot unchanged from the Silver Ghost. The 'Spirit of Ecstacy' figure was created by sculptor Charles Sykes. 'RR' monogram on the badge was red until 1933, black thereafter. Vertical radiator shutters can be adjusted by a knob on the dashboard to regulate the temperature.**

**Above: 1925 Phantom 1 tourer. This imposing vehicle, with simple lines and very little ornament, is a masterful piece of understated affluence. The price tag for a Phantom chassis alone, before it had received the coachbuilder's attentions, was something like eleven times the cost of an Austin Seven: bodywork could add half as much again. In addition to the**

**cars, like this one, manufactured at Derby in England, Phantoms were also built in the United States of America, at Springfield, Massachusetts. The majority of American-built examples had bodies by Brewster, an old established New York coachbuilding firm. Brewster bodies tended to reflect American taste in rather more flamboyant lines.**

# 1930 Bentley 4½ litre

A glorious chapter in the history of the British sports car is devoted to the cars W.O. Bentley built in the decade from 1921. Apprenticed as a steam locomotive engineer, Bentley worked on aero engine design during the first world war. The car he designed for production when peace returned owed rather more to pre-war light racing car practice than to the conventional road car design of the day. It was capable of speed and acceleration hitherto unknown in a road car of only 3 litres capacity, and massively robust construction, perhaps a legacy of Bentley's railway training, gave it durability to match. In the hands of the famous 'Bentley Boys', drivers like Woolf Barnato, J.D. Benjafield, Sammy Davis, and Bernard Rubin, Bentleys achieved a notable series of five wins in the tough Le Mans 24 hours race between 1924 and 1930.

## Specification

**Engine:** Four cylinders, in line. Bore 100mm (3.9in), stroke 140mm (5.5in), displacement 4398cc (268cu in). Shaft driven overhead camshaft. Roots type supercharger driven from crankshaft. Dual HT magneto ignition. Power output 182bhp.

**Transmission:** Four-speed gearbox, propeller shaft, live axle.

**Brakes:** Mechanically operated on all four wheels.

**Suspension:** Semi-elliptic leaf springs front and rear.

**Maximum speed:** 120mph (193km/h).

**Body:** Four-seater sports.

### The 'blower' Bentley

The original 3 litre four-cylinder sixteen-valve Bentley engine was enlarged to 4½ litres in search of power and greater flexibility when competitors began to catch up in 1928. The 4½ litre proved very amenable to tuning for racing. At the instigation of Clive Gallop and Tim Birkin, both of whom raced Bentleys, the brilliant young engineer Amherst Villiers was commissioned to design a supercharger ('blower') for the engine. Though Bentley himself was never entirely happy about the modification, which sacrificed some of the car's reliability for the gain in performance, it became a standard model for a time and was perhaps the most dramatic of the Bentleys. Victory at Le Mans eluded this version, though, despite its capacity for high speeds.

**Right: 4½ litre 'blower' Bentley. The Villiers supercharger protrudes beneath the radiator between the chassis dumb-irons, with a stoneguard over the twin SU carburetors which feed it. The short chassis and typically massive Bentley construction give the car a purposeful, solid appearance. To meet contemporary sports car racing regulations, Bentleys competed in the form shown, with four-seater bodywork and full road-going trim. During the 1930 season, while the factory progressed to racing the six-cylinder 6½ litre model, a team of three 4½ litre supercharged cars was entered by the Hon. Dorothy Paget at Brooklands, Le Mans, and in the Tourist Trophy and Irish Grand Prix. Birkin drove one, stripped of its fenders, to second place in the French Grand Prix. Shown here is a faithful replica of one of the Paget team cars.**

# 1930 MG M type Midget

To several generations of motoring enthusiasts, the marque MG has come to embody the quintessence of the sports car. On one hand, many of the great names of pre-war motor racing competed in MGs — Prince Bira, Dick Seaman, and George Eyston among them. The legendary Nuvolari won the 1933 Tourist Trophy race in a K3 Magnette. On the other hand, the MG Midgets, beginning with the M type shown here, opened up for the first time the market for a practical, inexpensive sports car: the M type cost £185 in 1930. Later Midgets, the TC in particular, spread the MG cult to the USA. The first MG of all, in 1924, had been the brainchild of Cecil Kimber, who ran the retail branch of the Morris company ('MG' stands for Morris Garages') in Oxford. Kimber had begun by adapting a Morris Cowley for use in reliability trials. These events, in which the principal element was the climbing of steep, muddy, often rocky tracks and byways, formed an important part of the British motor sport scene. MGs, nothing if not versatile, continued to be successful here as well as in international racing and record breaking.

**Specification:**

**Engine:** Four cylinders, in line. Bore 57 mm (2.2 in), stroke 83 mm (3.3 in), displacement 847 cc (52 cu in). Shaft driven overhead camshaft. Coil ignition. Power output 20 bhp at 4000 rpm.

**Transmission:** Three-speed gearbox, propeller shaft, live axle.

**Brakes:** Mechanically operated drum brakes on all four wheels.

**Suspension:** Semi-elliptic leaf springs front and rear.

**Wheelbase:** 1981 mm (6 ft 6 in).

**Maximum speed:** 65 mph (105 km/h).

**Body:** Two-seater sports, lightweight fabric covered construction.

**Left:** The little overhead camshaft engine, just over 8 hp on the old RAC rating, was borrowed from the contemporary Morris Minor, as were most of the M type's other mechanical components. It retained a single carburetor, though more highly tuned versions, including supercharged units for racing, were to follow.

**Above right:** This superbly restored M type, a 1930 model, shows the leather-cloth covered body construction adopted for lightness and low cost. In a diminutive package, the looks of this first Midget combined everything a sports car ought to be for the young enthusiast of the day. Visible between the front wheel and chassis is one of the friction type shock absorbers used before hydraulic dampers became common.

**Right:** The octagonal MG badge came to be a famous symbol of sporting motoring, and has survived all the ups and downs of the parent Morris company's mergers, takeovers, and eventual absorption into the present day British Leyland complex.

### The first MG Midget

In 1928, Morris launched a new small car, the 847cc Minor, which provided the basis for the MG M type introduced in the same year. The engine was a Wolseley design, acquired when Sir William Morris (later Lord Nuffield) took over the bankrupt Wolseley concern in 1927, and its origins can be traced back to the Hispano-Suiza aero engines Wolseley built during World War 1. The overhead camshaft, an unusual feature for a small, mass-produced power unit at the time, was driven from the crankshaft through bevel gears by a vertical shaft at the front of the cylinder block. The vertical shaft also carried the dynamo armature, a neat combination of functions but sometimes troublesome as oil interfered with the operation of the dynamo.

In standard form, the engine was fed by a single carburetor and developed a modest 20 bhp. Other Morris Minor features inherited by the M type were the small brakes and a wide ratio three-speed gear box. Possibly, this is not a very exciting specification on paper: but the small size and light weight of the machine helped to give it a brisk, responsive feel. It looked every inch a sports car. and enthusiasts loved it. Some 3,200 M types were built between 1928 and 1932, when it was replaced by the twin carburetor J2.

The MG policy of participation in racing soon led to the evolution of more highly tuned versions, some of them reduced in capacity to suit the 750cc international class limit. M types won the team prize in the 1930 Brooklands Double Twelve Hour race. Eyston achieved a record speed of 103 mph in a supercharged Midget at Montilhéry in 1931, winning a battle with Austin to be the first to produce a 100 mph 750cc car. The J2 Midget had improvements to the chassis, brakes, gearbox and engine, benefitting from competition experience.

# 1933 Aston Martin

When Lionel Martin installed a Coventry Simplex engine in a small Isotta-Fraschini chassis and so built himself a 'special' to drive in motoring competitions shortly before the 1914-18 war, he combined his own name with that of a popular hill-climb venue of the day, Aston Clinton, near Aylesbury, Buckinghamshire, and called the car an Aston Martin, coining a name which has remained associated with distinguished sports cars to this day. War delayed his plans, but the first production Aston Martins began to appear, in very small numbers, after 1920. The side valve engined road cars were refined and meticulously well made, and a successful overhead camshaft racing version was developed, financed and sometimes driven by the wealthy motoring enthusiast Count Zborowski. But sound engineering alone does not ensure commercial success: the money ran out, and in 1926 Aston Martin was acquired by Renwick and Bertelli. The latter designed a new car retaining the high quality of the old, but with a more advanced specification and a lower price. Production of two versions, the single carburetor standard model and the twin carburetor International, got under way gradually, speeding up after the move to a new factory at Feltham in 1930. Participation in racing helped development, and the Aston began to acquire a reputation for high performance and roadworthiness. Although of only 1½ litres capacity, the cars consistently gained very creditable placings behind larger engined opposition in the Le Mans 24 hour race between 1931 and 1937, in commemoration of which the twin carburetor car was called the Le Mans model after 1933.

## Aston Martin 1½ litre engine

At the heart of Bertelli's design was the engine, a four-cylinder single overhead camshaft unit with some unconventional details. It produced 70bhp in Le Mans form, and efficient cooling and lubrication systems allowed it to be driven indefinitely at 4000rpm, equivalent to a speed of over 70mph in top gear, and to reach 5000rpm for short periods. Although arranged side-by-side in each cylinder, rather than in line along the engine, the valves were all inclined at the same angle, resulting in wedge shaped combustion chambers. International and Le Mans versions had dry sump lubrication, with the oil stored in a tank remote from the engine. This feature, not unknown in racing cars but extremely rare on a road machine, ensured adequate oil cooling, maintained uninterrupted lubrication during very hard cornering, and allowed the engine to be mounted lower in the car, thus increasing stability.

**Above:** the 1½ litre Le Mans engine is fed by two SU carburetors. The circular blanking plate below them indicates the position occupied by the single carburetor on the earliest version of the engine, feeding into a passage cast in the cylinder block.

## Specification

**Engine:** Four cylinders, in line. Bore 69.3mm (2.7in), stroke 99mm (3.9in), displacement 1495cc (91cu in). Chain driven overhead camshaft. Twin SU carburetors. Magneto ignition. RAC rating 11.9hp. Power output 70bhp.

**Transmission:** Four-speed gearbox, propeller shaft, live axle.

**Brakes:** Cable operated drum brakes on all four wheels.

**Suspension:** Semi-elliptic leaf springs front and rear.

**Wheelbase:** 2161mm (8ft 7in).

**Maximum speed:** 85mph (137km/h).

**Body:** Two/four seater sports.

Above: low built and starkly functional, the Aston Martin Le Mans is every inch a sports car. The full-width touring windshield folds flat to reduce drag for high speed use, leaving individual aero screens to protect driver and passenger. A large slab tank at the rear carries $18\frac{1}{2}$ gallons of fuel. Enormous brake drums fill the wheels. This is the short chassis version, with a wheelbase of 2.2m (8ft 7in): for those requiring more spacious rear seat accommodation there was an alternative long chassis model with a 3m (10ft) wheelbase.

Left: the oil tank for the dry sump engine lubrication system is mounted between the dumb-irons at the front of the chassis, with a lever-action quick-release filler cap. Louvres in the fairing over the tank admit air to cool the oil.

# 1934 Talbot 105

Noteworthy among the more expensive British cars of the late twenties and early thirties were the Talbots produced by the London factory of the Anglo-French Sunbeam-Talbot-Darracq combine. Founded in 1903 as Clement-Talbot Ltd, the firm began by importing French Clement cars, but was building its own machines by 1906. In 1919 it was taken over by the British-owned but French-based Darracq company. Sunbeam was added to the family too, but the individual branches were to maintain separate indentities until the takeover by Rootes in 1935. Through the early twenties, Talbot struggled with a series of rather dated designs. But their fortunes took a turn for the better when the talented Swiss engineer, Georges Roesch, introduced a new 14/45hp car with a small six-cylinder engine in 1926. This 1665cc unit was enlarged to $2\frac{1}{4}$ litres to power the 75 and 90 models in 1930, and again to 3 litres for the 105 in 1931. With open sports bodywork and engine tuned by Fox and Nicholl, the Speed Model, rather unexpectedly, became a successful contender in sports car racing. With sporting sedan bodywork, like the 1934 105 shown here, the Talbot provided the wealthier motorist with a refined, high performance car.

**Above: sporting sedan. Well proportioned 'close coupled' four-door bodywork graces this 1934 Talbot 105. A high standard of finish allied to refined road manners and high performance made this a very sought after model, though it was not cheap. The long hood houses a quiet, powerful six-cylinder engine. Designer Georges Roesch took pride in keeping the external appearance of his engines as simple and uncluttered as possible: even multiple carburetors were shunned, in spite of which a very good power output was obtained. Large brake drums provide braking to match the car's speed.**

**Top:** large headlamps, carried on a sturdily braced cross tube, dominate the frontal appearance. Vertical slats control airflow to the radiator. The badge is composed of the arms of the Earl of Shrewsbury and Talbot, founder of the Clement-Talbot company, flanked by the words 'Talbot London'.

**Above:** study in a well-established style. The elegance of this Talbot is still very much in the vintage mode: as yet there is little hint of the onset of that conscious modernity which was to change car design, at least in external appearance, in the later years of the decade. 'Trafficators' — electric semaphore direction indicators, mounted in slots behind the rear doors — are one concession to progress. And there was nothing backward about Roesch's engineering, firmly in the forefront of its period, well ahead of many rivals, and still admired today for its quiet, almost understated accomplishment.

# 1950 Jaguar XK120

The sensation of the 1948 London Motor Show at Earls Court was the unveiling of the Jaguar XK 120. Though the pre-war SS 100 had provided a hint of the company's capability, few people were prepared for the impact of the new model. The sweeping lines of its full-width body redefined the popular image of a sports car overnight, banishing separate fenders and upright radiator grilles to nostalgic memory. Its specification sounded like something made in small numbers for the race track, not a production car intended for road use. Yet it had a surprisingly low price, comfortably under $3000 and much cheaper than some specialized cars of much less potential: indeed the question enthusiasts were to ask repeatedly about Sir William Lyons's Jaguars over the next fifteen years was 'How can he do it at the price?' With only pre-war sports cars to judge by, the sceptic could be forgiven for wondering about the claims made for the performance of the XK 120. But once production was under way, it began to prove itself in no uncertain terms. In 1949 on a stretch of Belgian motorway near Jabbeke regularly used for speed record runs, it recorded 126mph (202km/h) in standard trim. Numerous successes included Stirling Moss's victory in pouring rain in the 1950 Tourist Trophy. In 1952 at Montlhéry an XK 120 coupé averaged 100mph (160km/h) for a week.

Above: the racing successes of the XK engine were to make the Jaguar badge a famous emblem in sports car circles during the fifties and sixties.

## Specification

**Engine:** Six cylinders, in line. Bore 83mm (3.3in), stroke 106mm (4.2in), displacement 3442cc, (210cu in). Twin overhead camshafts, driven by two-stage roller chain, operate inclined valves in alloy cylinder head with hemispherical combustion chambers. Coil ignition. Power output 160bhp at 5200 rpm.

**Transmission:** Four-speed gearbox, propeller shaft, live axle.

**Brakes:** Hydraulically operated drum brakes on all four wheels.

**Suspension:** Front, independent by wishbones and torsion bars. Rear, semi-elliptic leaf springs.

**Wheelbase:** 2590mm (8ft 6in).

**Maximum speed:** 126mph (202km/h).

**Body:** Two-seater sports.

### The Jaguar XK engine

The engine of the XK 120, designed by William Heynes with help from Walter Hassan and cylinder head expert Harry Weslake, became one of the most celebrated sports car power units of all time. It was used in the XK 120, 140, 150 range, and then in the E type, it gave Jaguar five famous wins at Le Mans with the C type and D type as well as countless successes elsewhere, and it remains in production to this day for the XJ6. A six-cylinder unit of classic twin overhead camshaft type, it produced 160bhp in its original form but proved very amenable to tuning, around 300bhp being obtained from later racing versions. Rugged construction gave it reliability for long-distance racing: in road-going trim, less highly stressed, its longevity is legendary.

Above: the XK 120, first of a distinguished line of Jaguars, ushered in a new era in sports car design. Though the full-width body was new, Lyons skilfully adapted a reminiscence of the flowing wing line of a late vintage sports car to save it from the slab-sided, tank look which marred some other early full-width designs. Of more then 7500 XK 120's made, all but about 600 were exported. This particular car, NUB 120, was used by Ian Appleyard in becoming the first driver to win a Gold Cup for penalty-free runs in the demanding Alpine Rally for three consecutive years up to 1952. He also drove it to victory in the Tulip Rally and RAC Rally in 1951.

Left: driver's eye view, with the long, louvered hood ahead. The functional dashboard carries simple, round dials giving ample information including oil pressure and water temperature. On the left are two special instruments for rally time-keeping.

# Chapter
# 3 FRANCE

Though not among the pioneer companies involved in the earliest days of the automobile, Citroën emerged in the twenties and thirties as a major force in the French motor industry, providing cars of great dependability and keeping well to the fore in the adoption of new techniques. André Citroën had been an engineer with Mors, and started his own gear-cutting firm in 1913: the 'herring bone' symbol used on all Citroën cars derives from the bevel gears he made. The 1922 1½ litre type B2 shown here was a development of the first Citroën car, the type A of 1919. Plain and simple construction reflects Citroën's acquaintance with American mass-production methods. Disc wheels and bright paint contribute to the vehicle's engaging, almost toy-like appearance.

# 1902 Panhard

The transformation of the motor car from an inventor's experiment into something that could actually be manufactured and sold to the public was the work of a handful of companies operating in France and Germany in the last ten or fifteen years before the turn of the century. Most influential, perhaps, of these pioneers in setting the pattern for the future was Panhard et Levassor of Paris. For the système Panhard', adopted for all their cars from 1891, comprised a lengthways, front mounted engine driving rearwards through a central gearbox to the rear axle, prefiguring the layout which has remained the convention ever since, and has been seriously challenged only in recent years, by the growth in the number of transverse engined, front wheel drive designs. Panhard et Levassor, makers of woodworking machinery, had become involved with motor cars in 1887 through Edouard Sarazin. On Sarazin's death, the French manufacturing licence for Daimler engines passed to his widow.

**Above: veteran dashboard, with drip-feed lubricators much in evidence. Early cars demanded constant vigilance and understanding from the driver to avoid mechanical mishaps of one sort or another. Servicing, too, tended to be a never-ending task, with numerous oilers and greasers** **requiring attention on a more or less daily basis if the car was in regular use. Jobs like grinding in the valves, part of a major engine overhaul today, might well need doing every week or two to keep the motor running at all efficiently: a full-time chauffeur-mechanic was almost essential.**

## PANHARD

### Emile Levassor, motoring pioneer

Though the firm was called 'Panhard et Levassor' (which continued to be its official title right up to its absorption by Citroën in 1965, the last Panhard cars being made in 1967) it has always tended to be abbreviated to Panhard. But it was Emile Levassor, rather than his partner René Panhard, who was fascinated by the new motor car. His Belgian friend Sarazin had first interested him in making engines to the German Daimler design. The Daimler engine was a narrow angle V-twin which ran at what was then thought to be the very high speed of 750 to 800rpm, and it represented a significant step forward from the ponderous, slow running motor of the first commercially produced Benz car. But Levassor was less impressed with the rest of the Daimler car, a spidery, rear engined quadricycle which appeared at the Paris World Fair in 1889, and he began experimenting with designs of his own. The front engined layout he selected was the first step away from the top heavy mechanised dogcart form that the motor car had taken so far.

Levassor was not merely a motor car builder, he was a driver too. In the first ever motor race, from Paris to Bordeaux and back, in 1895, he covered the distance of 732 miles at an average speed of 15mph, driving single-handed for over 48 hours and finishing well ahead of his nearest rival. Epic city-to-city races on open roads continued to be organised until 1903, and Panhard cars were repeatedly successful. Racing led both to progressively larger and more powerful engines, a four-cylinder unit coming in 1896, and to the use of a wheel instead of a tiller for steering. Sadly, Levassor died in 1897, partly as a result of injuries sustained in the 1896 Paris — Marseilles race, won by another Panhard. A monument to this pioneer designer and racing driver stands at the Porte Maillot in Paris.

## Specification

**Engine:** Two cylinders, in line. Bore 90mm (3.5in), stroke 130mm (5.1in), displacement 1654cc (100cu in). Automatic inlet valves, side exhaust valves. Trembler coil ignition. Nominal horsepower rating .

**Transmission:** Cone clutch, three-speed sliding pinion gearbox, final drive by side chains to live axle.

**Brakes:** Footbrake on transmission, handbrake on rear wheels (externally contracting type).

**Suspension:** Semi-elliptic leaf springs front and rear.

**Body:** Four-seater tonneau.

**Above:** by the time this 7hp Panhard was built in 1902, the 'systeme Panhard', with a front mounted, vertical engine driving the back wheels, was well established and beginning to be widely copied. The hood and gilled tube radiator in front had put an end to the 'horseless carriage' look of the earliest cars, and the front and rear wheels were now of equal size. Other developments pioneered by the Panhard et Levassor company included the two shaft, sliding pinion gearbox, ancestor of almost all modern manual shift boxes. But veteran features like final drive by side chains, a chassis made of wood reinforced with metal 'flitch plates', non-removable wheels with shortlived tires, and oil lamps remained: only a hardy and resourceful motorist would undertake a long journey on such a machine on the roads of the day.

# 1903 De Dietrich

The Société Lorraine de Anciens Etablissements de Dietrich et Compagnie, the firm's full title, was already an old established industrial concern, famous for building railway locomotives, when it first began to produce motor cars in 1897. Rather than struggling with the development of new prototypes, the Baron Adrien de Turckheim chose to buy the rights to manufacture the models of existing car makers in the De Dietrich factories in northern France. To begin with, the designs were provided by Amédée Bollée the younger, whose family, including his father, Amédée senior, and brother, Léon, carried out important pioneer work, making cars under their own name in Le Mans. Then, around the turn of the century, a range of models originated by the Turcat-Méry company of Marseilles was adopted. The young Ettore Bugatti, later to become a celebrated car maker in his own right, also produced designs for De Dietrich in 1902, but the example shown here, a 1903 24hp model, is of the Turcat-Méry type. Léon Turcat and Simon Méry experimented with Panhard and Peugeot cars before designing their own, so the general layout, not surprisingly, follows the Panhard system, with the engine in front and final drive by side chains. Panhard-like, too, are the wooden chassis frame, reinforced with metal plates, and the gilled tube radiator, features which the contemporary German Mercedes models were beginning to make outdated. But the De Dietrich is not merely a copy: it simply illustrates how quickly certain conventions in car design became accepted as the established pattern.

## Racing influence

The De Dietrich company began to take part in racing very early on, and continued to do so for some years. Standard models were entered in events where there was a touring car class, and special lightweight competition versions were developed too. First on the racing scene were Bollée's sensational racing 'torpilleurs' (torpedoes), with bodywork the shape of an inverted boat, followed by lightened versions of the Turcat-Méry designed cars. Early racing rules defined classes simply by the weight of the vehicle, with no limit on engine size, so firms like De Dietrich, Panhard, and Mors fitted larger and larger engines in flimsy frames carrying the scantiest of bodywork in the quest for higher speeds. Though the 1903 24hp car was designed and built as a tourer, the size of its engine (5.4 litres) reflects the lessons learned with the racers: indeed, the whole car is not unlike the 16hp version run successfully in the Paris — Vienna race of 1902.

**Above: final drive to the wooden-spoked rear wheels is by side chains from a countershaft at the back of the gearbox. The double curved rear fender covers both wheel and chain. Abrasive dust and grit thrown up from the rough roads of the period must have led to rapid chain wear.**

### Specification

**Engine:** Four cylinders, in line. Bore 120mm (4.7in), stroke 120mm (4.7in), displacement 5428cc (331cu in). Automatic inlet valves, side exhaust valves. Low tension magneto ignition. Nominal horsepower rating, 24.

**Transmission** Cone clutch, four-speed sliding pinion gearbox, final drive by side chains to live axle.

**Brakes:** Footbrake on transmission, handbrake on rear wheels (externally contracting type).

**Suspension:** Semi-elliptic leaf springs front and rear.

**Body:** Four-seater tonneau with victoria top.

Above: with its flared fenders, angled to deflect spray away from the occupants, its polished oil lamps, and the luxurious buttoned leather upholstery of its high set seats, the De Dietrich is an impressive sight. The victoria top keeps some rain off rear seat occupants, but it must form an alarming wind trap, for the only windshield effect is provided by chauffeur and front seat passenger! There is an obvious joint between the front and rear sections of the bodywork: with the rear portion demounted, leaving only the front seats, the car would take on the stark appearance of the contemporary racing machines, with only a fuel tank and spare tires strapped on at the back.

Left: entrance to the tonneau compartment is through a rear door, the central portion of the seat folding to allow access. The top has an opening curtain as well, and a step is thoughtfully provided to assist in climbing into this elevated carriage.

# 1903 Georges Richard

The technical history of the early motor car, the struggles of the pioneer car builders to overcome the many problems by which they were beset, the emergence of current automobile practice from among the many short-lived experiments, forms a fascinating study. While racing had helped to breed ever larger and more powerful machines, the light car, 'voiturette' in French, had continued to develop, growing in reliability and practicality because its designers learned from their experience, as this little 10hp Georges Richard of 1903 shows. But technicalities are not the whole story. This car marks no great mechanical breakthrough, though it is a competent design of its period. What it has is a charm and character which emphasise how quickly the motor car became more than just an exercise in engineering.

### Richard, Brasier, and Unic

The motor cars of Georges Richard were a product, as were those of many other early makers, of expertise garnered from a number of sources. His first effort, in 1897, was a belt drive vehicle similar to the contemporary Benz. Then three years later came a light voiturette built under licence from the Belgian Vivinus concern. In 1902 Richard was joined by Brasier, who had previously designed successful cars for Mors, and this partnership produced a range of models, between 10 and 40hp, broadly of the Panhard type. The smaller versions, like the 10hp car shown here, had a tubular metal chassis, and chain final drive had given way to a shaft. The sliding pinion gearbox gave direct drive in top, one of the first examples of this now almost universal feature. The paths of the two partners diverged again after a few years. Cars built to Brasier's design won the Gordon Bennett Trophy races in France in 1904 and 1905. Subsequently known simply as Brasier, that branch of the business continued to produce cars until 1930. Georges Richard, meanwhile, renamed his company Unic, and went on to suppy a large proportion of the taxis to be seen on the streets of both Paris and London.

**Left: early car manufacturers adopted and modified the body styles of the existing coachbuilding industry. In the case of this car, rescued from a British breaker's yard in Sussex, the process was repeated when, during restoration, it was fitted with the landaulette body from a horse-drawn brougham. Thrupp and Maberly, makers of the body, went on from carriages to become famous builders of high quality car bodies, so the combination is an appropriate one. Closed sedan cars began to appear very early on, as it was realized that the driver no longer needed to talk to the horses, but their practicality and popularity was to some extent limited by the fact that it took a long time for any form of windshield wiper to be contrived.**

## Specification

**Engine:** Two cylinders, in line. Bore 90mm (3.5in), stroke 110mm (4.3in), displacement 1396cc (85cu in). Automatic inlet valves, side exhaust valves. Coil ignition. Nominal horse-power rating, 10.

**Transmission:** Cone clutch, three-speed sliding pinion gearbox (with direct drive top gear), propeller shaft, live axle.

**Brakes:** Footbrake on transmission, handbrake on rear wheels.

**Suspension:** Semi-elliptic leaf springs front and rear.

**Body:** Two-seater landaulette.

**Above:** lofty proportions combined with a short wheelbase give this 1903 Georges Richard 10hp a distinctive 'top hat' look, full of character. The low-slung mounting of the tube radiator at the front leaves the neat little hood uncluttered.

**Far left:** the hood hinges up in one piece to reveal a vertical, in line twin cylinder engine of De Dion design. An inlet manifold fabricated from brass pipe conveys the mixture to each cylinder from an updraft carburetor (one through which the air flows in an upwards direction, common on early engines but nowadays entirely superseded by sidedraft and downdraft designs). Each cylinder head is furnished with a tap through which fuel can be squirted to prime the engine for starting from cold. Contemporary manuals also recommended injecting a little kerosene at the end of a day's run to prevent pistons and valves from sticking, a possibility in an era of primitive fuel and lubricant technology.

**Left:** 'Conduite intérieur', interior drive, as the French called sedan cars. The driving compartment of the Georges Richard has plenty of pedals and levers to keep the driver occupied.

# 1906 Renault

In 1898 Louis Renault built his first car in a garden shed in the Paris suburb of Billancourt, putting the engine from a De Dion tricycle into a little four-wheeler. Like many other young men at the time, he was full of enthusiasm for the new automobile. The company he founded with his brothers Marcel and Fernand has subsequently grown to be one of the major names in the industry. For even Renault's earliest car was successful: demonstrating it to friends, he drove them one at a time up the hill to Montmartre, the highest part of Paris, winning orders for replicas at once. In 1906, when the car shown here was built, Louis Renault was made a Chevalier de la Légion d'Honneur as a 'captain of industry'. The Renault organisation, now state-owned, still has a factory at Billancourt, and Louis Renault's garden shed is preserved there.

## Specification

**Engine:** Four cylinders, in line, ir two blocks of two. Bore 100mm (3.9in), stroke 140mm (5.5in), displacement 4399cc (268cu in). Side valves, L heads. HT magneto ignition. Maker's rating 20/30hp; RAC rating 24.8hp.

**Transmission:** Cone clutch, four-speed gearbox, propeller shaft, live axle.

**Brakes:** Footbrake on transmission, handbrake on rear wheels.

**Suspension:** Semi-elliptic leaf springs, front. Semi-elliptic and transverse leaf springs, rear.

**Body:** Limousine.

Left, below: the four cylinder engine has the cylinders grouped in two blocks of two. Typical of engines of the period are the two caps screwed into the top of each cylinder to provide access to the side mounted valves when required, necessary because the two cylinder blocks were each cast in one piece without a removable head. One of each pair of caps also provides a mounting for a sparking plug. The brass pipe inlet manifold runs from a carburetor on the far side of the engine, hidden in this view. Cooling water pipes are brass, too. The radiator is mounted to the rear of the engine, against the dashboard, a layout which remained a feature of all Renault models until around 1930.

Right: spare tire is fitted to a rim which can be clamped alongside the existing wheel. This eased the problem of punctures, which had previously necessitated an infuriating struggle to remove and refit a tough, inflexible tire with the wheel in situ. Easily removable complete wheels were yet to become a general feature.

Below: the confidence and assurance reflected in the handsome bearing of this 1906 20/30hp Renault show clearly how far the motor car had progressed beyond the tentative, experimental stage of its development.

# 1924 Bugatti type 35

In the annals of car designers and builders, a special place is reserved for Ettore Bugatti. Born in Italy, but working in France, he was an artist and craftsman to whom engineering was a matter of genius, intuition, and enthusiasm. Without elaborate theory and mathematics, he had an almost infallible instinct for structural fitness, proportion, and economy of material which complemented an original, inventive mind and acute powers of observation. The result is that a Bugatti car, this type 35 for example, has all the harmony, the unity of purpose, design, and material, of a fine artefact. The methods of construction proceed from techniques of meticulous craftsmanship in a factory without elaborate mass-production tooling. Like any product strongly stamped with the personality of one man, it is not without idiosyncrasy. But to anyone with a scrap of responsive spirit it is a thing of beauty.

## The first production racer

The type 35 was the car which established Bugatti's mastery. Its conception was unique at the time: a racing car, but one which could be produced and sold to amateur drivers on a commercial scale. It had numerous successes in racing, at Grand Prix level, yet it could also double as a road car. Racers in the twenties still had a second seat to carry a mechanic and, if necessary, skimpy fenders and lighting equipment could be added.

The type 35 engine is typical of Bugatti practice, with roller and ball bearings for the crankshaft and big-ends. The two blocks of four cylinders have non-removable heads, and there are three valves, two inlet and one exhaust, per cylinder. The crankcase to which the two blocks are fitted is bolted rigidly into the chassis which it helps to stiffen. The whole unit is superbly finished, perfect fits eliminating the need for gaskets.

The list of drivers who raced type 35s is a formidable roll-call, including among many others Benoist, Campbell, Chiron, Dreyfus, Etancelin, Eyston, and Nuvolari. And enthusiastic owners still compete in 35s today, notably at the Bugatti Owners' Club Prescott hill climb.

**Left: The tapering tail of the type 35 forms part of the classic racing car shape, a blend of function and beauty not often equalled. Two seats are provided, but elbows will stick out! The tail neatly covers the forward-pointing quarter-elliptic leaf springs of the unusual but effective rear suspension, and also houses a 100 litre fuel tank. Brake drums are integral with the alloy wheels, a Bugatti patent. Notice how the line of bolts on the body panel is lock-wired for security, typical of the meticulous attention to detail that went into these cars. In the cockpit, the magneto, driven from the rear end of the engine camshaft, protrudes through the centre of the mottled alloy dash panel, so ignition advance and retard is easily adjusted.**

Above: The slim, elegant horseshoe radiator was a Bugatti trademark. Below it, the front axle is a polished, hollow forging, strong but light, exemplifying Bugatti's craftsmanlike approach.

This is the type 35 in its original form. Other versions that were to appear included the supercharged type 35B, distinguished by a slightly broader radiator, and the type 35A, sometimes called the 'Tecla', with a less highly tuned engine for those not requiring out-and-out racing performance. Also, engines of several different capacities were produced for racing.

Above: The gearlever and handbrake are outside on the right, the former projecting through a slot in the bodywork. Behind the handbrake is a radius arm locating the rear axle.

### Specification

**Engine:** Eight cylinders, in line, in two blocks of four. Bore 66 mm (2.6 in), stroke 88 mm (3.5 in), displacement 1991 cc (121 cu in). Shaft driven overhead camshaft. HT magneto ignition. Power output approximately 90 bhp at 5500 rpm.

**Transmission:** Multi plate wet clutch, four-speed gearbox, propeller shaft, live axle.

**Brakes:** Cable operated on all four wheels, drums integral with alloy wheels.

**Suspension:** Front, semi-elliptic leaf springs passing through forged axle. Rear, reversed quarter-elliptic leaf springs and radius rods.

**Wheelbase:** 2400 mm (7 ft 10.5 in)

**Maximum speed:** at least 100 mph (160 km/h).

**Body:** Two-seater sports racing.

# 1938 Citroën 7cv 'Traction Avant'

This rakish, sporty roadster version of the celebrated Citroen 'Traction' has an immediate nostalgic appeal. Perhaps even more than the better-known sedan model, which was part of the French scene for longer, it is evocative of its era, unmistakeably stamped with the style of the thirties. Paradoxically, though, its significance lies less in nostalgia than in innovation. For at its introduction in 1934 the innovatory design of the 'Traction' put it firmly in the avant garde of automobile engineering. The boldness of his decision underlined by the economic difficulties of the time, André Citroën chose front wheel drive and unitary ('chassis-less') body construction. Both features were then virtually unknown in mass-produced cars, but both, of course, are part of the accepted standard pattern for European cars today.

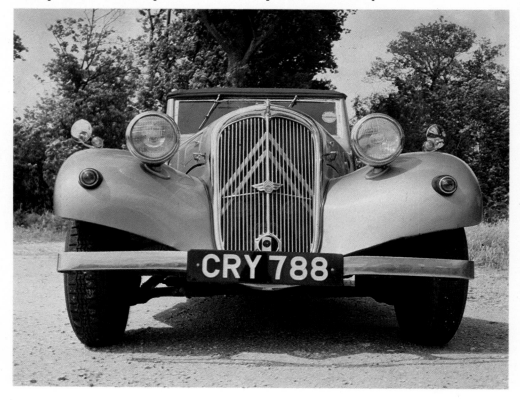

### Citroën's pioneering design

The company referred to the cars simply by their taxable horsepower rating — 7CV (1628 cc) and 11CV (1911 cc), or 12 and 15 under the RAC system in Britain. A 15CV six-cylinder 2867 cc version appeared in 1938. But the public quickly adopted the design's outstanding feature as its title: 'Traction Avant' — French for 'front wheel drive' — was soon abbreviated to 'Traction'. Cord in the USA had pointed the way: Adler in Germany and Grégoire in France had used front wheel drive too. But Citroën was the first to adopt it for a truly mass-produced car. The advantages of good roadholding and a low, unobstructed floor line quickly proved their worth: all subsequent Citroëns have had front wheel drive. The faithful 'Traction' remained in production until 1957, by which time some 750,000 had been made. But other companies were slow to follow suit until the sixties and seventies.

Citroëns other innovation much more construction, in which the bodyshell, welded up from steel pressings, formed a self-supporting, integral structure with no separate chassis frame, developed from the work of the American Budd company. It was a natural progression from the practice, already established, of using pressed steel panels for a separate body. Properly engineered, it provides a lighter, stronger, cheaper car than any other avilable mass-production method. In consequence, almost all large-scale manufacturers had adopted it by the early post-war years.

Far left: Citroëns were assembled at Slough in England as well as at the main factory in Paris. Righthand drive marks this as a Slough-built example. The direction indicators on this car are a later addition, though sedan models were in production late enough in France to get into the 'winker' era. Behind the elegant, traditional radiator grille and separate headlamps is a car of notably advanced design for its date, details like hydraulic brakes and torsion bar suspension complementing the major innovations in layout.

## Specification

**Engine:** Four cylinders, in line, wet liners. Bore 72 mm (2.8 in), stroke 100 mm (3.9 in), displacement 1628 cc (99 cu in). Pushrod operated overhead valves. Coil ignition. Power output 36 bhp.

**Transmission:** Three-speed gearbox, front wheel drive.

**Brakes:** Hydraulic on all four wheels.

**Suspension:** Front, independent, torsion bars. Rear, beam axle, torsion bars.

**Wheelbase:** 2908 mm (9 ft 6.5 in).

**Maximum speed:** 65 mph (105 km/h).

**Body:** Two-door roadster with rumble (dickey) seat, integral structure.

Left: Room for two friends, weather permitting! The dickey seat (in Britain) or rumble seat (in America), providing occasional extra passenger accommodation, was often incorporated in two-seater roadsters and coupes of the period, an ingenious ploy in the perennial conflict between practicality and the desire to look sporty. The style failed to reappear after World War II, but finds an echo in the 'two-plus-two' formula, difficult access and all.

Below: The roadster was perhaps the most stylish form in which the 'Traction' appeared. This and the related fixed head coupe formed the sporting end of the range: the bread-and-butter models were four-door sedans in several permutations, including an eight or nine seater, its length emphasised by the low build characteristic of all the family. The car shown is a 1938 7CV model and so has the shortest of three wheelbase dimensions found in the range.

# 4 GERMANY

It is generally accepted that the motor car, in practical form, first made its appearance in Germany. But engineers in other countries, notably France, quickly took up the work of Benz and Daimler, and the story became an international one, with Germany's industry developing alongside those elsewhere in Europe and America. From Germany were to come Mercedes and Porsche cars — both in their different ways to achieve distinction by superb engineering and great success in motor sport — and the Volkswagen phenomenon. First to adopt mass-production in Germany was Opel, which became one of the first footholds of the now strong American influence in the European industry. Shown here is a 1931 Opel 1.8 litre saloon.

# 1904 Mercedes 28/32hp

Mercedes is celebrated as one of the great names in the history of the motor industry, so it is perhaps surprising to learn that it was never the name of a company. For Mercedes cars were the product of the German Daimler firm, founded in 1890. Although the other German pioneer, Carl Benz, was first actually to produce cars for sale to the public, Gottlieb Daimler's work in translating into practicality the principle of the four-stroke internal combustion engine had been of great import, and when he began to make cars they were clearly in advance of those of Benz. Among the wealthy enthusiasts who bought Daimler cars was Emile Jellinek, business man and Consul-General of the Austro-Hungarian empire in Nice. After Daimler's death in 1900, his assistant Wilhelm Maybach took over as designer and was persuaded by Jellinek to introduce a new model, less unwieldy than the $5\frac{1}{2}$ litre heavyweight which the Daimler had become. For Jellinek not only drove Daimlers, he also sold them to his friends in France. To overcome anti-German prejudice in France, and to avoid legal conflict with Daimler licence holders Panhard et Levassor, he called the cars he sold after his daughter, Mercédès. The new model made a distinguished debut in the motoring competitions of Nice week, 1901, and soon began to outperform the previously unchallenged French cars, Panhard, Mors, and Peugeot, in racing. Sales quickly reflected this success, and in 1902 the Daimler company adopted Mercedes as a brand name for its cars. By now, Jellinek had a seat on the board of directors of the Daimler company, as well as exclusive sales rights in Austro-Hungary, Germany, Belgium, and France, and he often called himself Jellinek-Mercedes. His involvement lasted until 1908, when he resigned his directorship, having previously given up his sales licences in 1905. Maybach left Daimler in 1907 to found his own company, making a series of large and luxurious cars during the succeeding years, as well as developing aero engines including those used in the Zeppelin airships. But the departure of the two men in no way hindered the progress of the Mercedes marque. Paul Daimler, son of Gottlieb, returned from Austro-Daimler in Vienna to the Mercedes factory at Stuttgart to succeed Maybach as designer, and both distinguished road cars and successful racing machines continued to be produced after the first world war.

## Towards the modern motor car

From the 1901 design produced by Maybach at Jellinek's request, the Daimler company developed a range of models designated Mercedes Simplex which have been hailed as the 'first modern motor cars'. They combined for the first time features like pressed steel chassis sidemembers, good brakes, a gate type gearshift, a honeycomb radiator, an engine with mechanical inlet valves, and magneto ignition, which were widely copied and became general practice thereafter. None of these items was in itself completely new, but putting them all together in one design added up to an innovation. Perhaps most important were the changes affecting the engine. Camshaft operated inlet valves, instead of the earlier atmospheric or 'automatic' ones which simply opened against a spring in response to the vacuum created by the descending piston, meant that valve timing could be predetermined and controlled. Electric ignition in place of the hot tube system meant that ignition timing was similarly controllable. In conjunction with an improved carburetor, these developments made it possible to run the engine over a wide range of speeds, controlled by the throttle as in a modern car. Compared with earlier machines, which had tended to run at a constant speed in each gear with only a limited measure of control, the flexibility and responsiveness of the new Mercedes was a revelation to drivers of the day. Handling and braking were improved to match. Clearly, the motor car had moved out of its first, primitive, phase: coachbuilders began to create body styles specifically for it, no longer merely adapting horse-drawn types. The scene was set for the arrival of the grand, ostentatious cars built for the wealthy in the decade preceeding the first world war.

Above: this 1904 28/32hp model is a clear assertion of the new-found confidence and technical accomplishment of the Mercedes Simplex cars. Gone are the wooden chassis and tube radiator of the early days. Gone, too, is the rear-entrance tonneau body. Coachbuilders Rothschild of Paris began the trend to side entrance styles with the first of a much-copied line of 'Roi de Belges' bodies on a 1903 60hp Mercedes, and this double phaeton reflects the new pattern.

Top left: throttle and ignition control quadrants are mounted in the centre of a polished, wood-rimmed steering wheel.

Top right: all the bright work on this superbly restored car is spotless. Oil side lamps are of American manufacture.

Bottom left: gas headlamps are fed by rubber pipe from a carbide-and-water acetylene generator. A handle on top makes them easily removable from the mounting fork for cleaning.

Bottom right: toccata and fugue? An organ-like array of oilers, each with a little sight glass, confronts the driver: the lubrication system was still somewhat elementary and far from unobtrusive in 1904. A brass plate lists Daimler patents. The switchgear is in brass, too, and a clock is provided.

# 1908 Benz 120hp

The history of motor racing is very nearly as old as the motor car itself. Almost as soon as there were two cars to race against each other, enthusiasts were racing them, and very quickly it became an important matter of prestige for any company interested in selling cars to compete successfully in racing. So the manufacturers soon began to develop special cars for racing. The unrestrictive rules under which early races were run made the recipe a simple one: the largest possible engine was fitted to the lightest possible chassis, there were four wheels, two seats (racers carried a mechanic as well as the driver until about 1925), a fuel tank, and very little else. After the end of the long distance city-to-city races in 1903, the courses used were still ordinary roads, but now they were closed to normal traffic for the duration of the race. For example, the 1908 Grand Prix (the title was at first only used for French events) was run over ten laps of 48 mile (77km) circuit near Dieppe. The days of the French domination of racing were over, and the race was a fierce battle between the German Benz and Mercedes teams. Hémery, on a Benz of the type shown here, finished second to Lautenschlager on a Mercedes after being delayed when a stone smashed his goggles. Speeds of up to 100mph (160km/h) were reached in the race, and the spectacle must indeed have been stirring.

## Last of the GP giants

1908 was the last year of the giant cars in Grand Prix racing. There were no Grands Prix between 1909 and 1911, and when they resumed, more complicated regulations and a more scientific approach raised a new breed of smaller engined racers. Indeed, some attempt at restriction had already been made in 1908, with a maximum bore size of 155mm for a four-cylinder engine and a minimum weight limit of 1100kg (2424lbs). Within these limits, Benz produced a car with a capacity of more than 3 litres in each of its cylinders. It is an interesting index of progress that such an engine was needed to produce around 120bhp, a power output which is today within the reach of a production car of, say, 2½ litres or a 750cc racing motorcycle.

**Above: final drive is by chain to the wooden spoked rear wheel. The driving sprockets, the handbrake and gearlever are all drilled for lightness. Tires are fitted to removable rims.**

### Specification

**Engine:** Four cylinders, in line, in two blocks of two. Bore 155mm (6.1in), stroke 165mm (6.5in), displacement 12455cc (760cu in). Pushrod operated overhead valves. Dual HT magneto ignition. Power output approximately 120bhp at 1650rpm.

**Transmission:** Cone clutch, four-speed gearbox with integral differential, final drive by side chains.

**Brakes:** Rear wheels only.

**Suspension:** Semi-elliptic leaf springs front and rear.

**Wheelbase:** 2769mm (9ft 1in).

**Maximum speed:** 100mph (160km/h).

**Body:** Two-seater racing.

Above: the 1908 12½ litre 120hp Grand Prix Benz is a splendid survivor from the age of giant racers. White was the German national racing color. Because chain drive allows the differential to be mounted on the chassis, and there are no front brakes, the axles are light (low unsprung weight) in relation to the weight of the car, allowing comparatively soft springs to be used and helping to provide a less damaging ride and better roadholding than might be expected from a machine with such a large engine. Nevertheless, it must have taken considerable muscle power on the part of the driver to hurl a car like this round a bumpy, winding course at an average speed of 60 or 70mph (100 or 115 km/h) during a race lasting six or seven hours.

Right: driver's eye view. There are two brake pedals, operating band brakes on the countershaft so that the wheels are slowed through the driving chains and sprockets. Gauge measures air pressure in the fuel tank.

# 1912 Opel 5/14

The most successful and popular small cars made in Germany in the period before the first world war were Opels, like this 5/14 model of 1912/13. While Daimler and Benz made large and expensive cars, it was left to Opel to supply the less wealthy sector of the market, and, like Morris in England, to begin the move towards mass-production. Adam Opel AG was already an old-established firm making sewing machines and bicycles when they began to build Lutzmann cars in 1898. Primitive design limited the appeal of these machines, and the company switched to licence-built Darracqs between 1902 and 1905, while developing their own designs at the same time. The setback of a factory fire in 1911 was turned to good advantage when it provided an opportunity to update production techniques.

**Above: control layout is typical of the period. The upper section of the two-piece windshield can be angled or opened as required.**

**Above: acetylene gas headlamps flank the radiator, all in polished brass. The whole car creates an impression of neat, simple, effective design.**

**Right: this Opel 5/14, from the company's own collection, is an appealing little car, its blue paint nicely complemented by polished brasswork. A small hood contributes to the pleasing proportions of the two-seater body. The rumble seat folds down out of sight into the tail section when not required. Detachable wheels facilitate tire changing, and the spare can be carried on the righthand running board because the outside brake and gear levers preclude a driver's door. The brass fuel tank is visible under the rear of the car. The kind of effective, uncomplicated design which is represented by this model, simple to build and reliable in service, enabled Opel to become Germany's principal supplier of small and medium size cars, though they built larger** vehicles as well. The company consolidated its position between the wars, becoming the first German concern to install an American-style production line for car production in 1924. They realized the importance, too, of establishing a nationwide service organisation, with a system of standard repair charges. By 1928 Opel was the country's largest car manufacturer. The Opel family had continued to be closely involved in the company — Fritz von Opel's enthusiasm for high-speed motoring led him to experiment with a rocket-propelled car in 1927 — but in the increasing economic difficulties of the late twenties the majority of the shares were bought by the General Motors of America combine.

# 1925 Austro-Daimler

For the first seven years of its existence, Austro-Daimler was simply an Austrian subsidiary of the German Daimler company, building cars to early Daimler designs in Vienna. Independence, both in financial matters and engineering, came in 1906, and the firm was fortunate in securing the services of Ferdinand Porsche, one of the ablest and most inventive automobile engineers of all time. The car he designed in 1910, intended for success in the Prince Henry touring car trials, brought the company considerable acclaim, winning the competition handsomely. It had an overhead camshaft 5.7 litre engine which pointed the way for later sports car designers. After the first world war, Porsche and Austro-Daimler continued with a large, fast tourer, its advanced 4.2 litre engine constructed largely in light alloy. Scaling down this design produced the ADM series, introduced in 1924, an example of which is shown here. This proved to be another successful model, and after Porsche had moved on to work for Daimler its development was continued by his former assistant, Karl Rabe. The resulting 3 litre ADM 111 version was a 100mph car. In short-chassis form it won Austro-Daimler the team prize in the 1928 TT race.

**Above: distinctively shaped Austro-Daimler radiator carries this name plate, its style echoing, perhaps, the fashion of the 1910/11 era when the marque first came to prominence in the Prince Henry Alpine trials.**

Above: a deeply curved front axle added to the individual character of the car. Visible here are the front brakes: four wheel braking was beginning to be more general by this time, though still resisted by some manufacturers and drivers.

Left: stylish vintage sporting tourer. This 1925 type **ADM/BK 19/70hp** Austro-Daimler, sometimes called the Alpine Sports model, is an impressive example of what the best car makers of the period could achieve by refining a well-established style to produce a design functional and simple in appearance, yet full of character and purpose. Porsche's overhead camshaft engine endowed the car with performance to match its looks. Like Lanchester and Rolls-Royce, Austro-Daimler fitted long, cantilever rear springs to smooth the progress over rough, Alpine roads.

### Specification

**Engine:** Six cylinders, in line. Bore 71.5mm (2.8in), stroke 110mm (4.3in), displacement 2650cc (162cu in). Single overhead camshaft. HT magneto ignition. Maker's rating 19/70hp.
amshaft. HT magneto ignition. Maker's rating 19/70hp.

**Transmission:** Four-speed gearbox, propeller shaft, live axle.

**Brakes:** Mechanically operated drum brakes on all four wheels.

**Suspension:** Semi-elliptic leaf springs, front. Cantilever leaf springs, rear.

**Maximum speed:** 70mph (113km/h).

**Body:** Five-seater tourer.

# 1953 VW Beetle

This is an early export version of the Volkswagen Beetle, a car which has a fair claim to be regarded as one of the most remarkable automobiles of all time. In numbers produced it is unequalled: it surpassed the Ford model T's record in 1972, when European production ceased at the end of 1977 around 20 million had been made, and it is still manufactured elsewhere. It is familiar the world over, its exploits are legion and its durability legendary. Ferdinand Porsche approached the creation of a low-cost, rugged people's car ('Volkswagen') with typical originality, choosing unconventional designs for the prototypes built right back in 1938. Air cooling and a rear engine equipped it to cope with almost any terrain and climate, its high top gear made it virtually unburstable, and its tough dependability won the admiration of countless drivers.

**Specification**

**Engine:** Four cylinders, horizontally opposed. Bore 75mm (2.9in), stroke 64mm (2.5in), displacement 1131cc (69cu in). Pushrod operated overhead valves. Coil ignition. Power output 25bhp at 3300rpm.

**Transmission:** Four-speed gearbox in unit with differential, swinging half axles.

**Brakes:** Drums on all four wheels.

**Suspension:** Front, independent, trailing arms, torsion bars. Rear, independent, swing axles, torsion bars.

**Wheelbase:** 2400mm (7ft 10.5in).

**Maximum speed:** 62mph (100km/h).

**Body:** Four-seater two-door sedan.

Left: with a rear-mounted engine and no radiator, there is nothing to interrupt the smooth, aerodynamic curve of the front end. Under the front lid (called bonnet, boot or hood according to choice by Beetle owners) are housed the fuel tank and spare wheel as well as some luggage space. The windshield, like the rear window, grew larger as the years passed. The badge carries the emblem of Wolfsburg, the town largely created round the Volkswagen factory.

Far left: the rear window is one index of the continual evolution of the Beetle throughout its production life. This is already one stage on from the original version which had a central bar dividing the window into two halves, and it was to undergo several increases in size in later years. The compact flat-four engine fits neatly into the tail. Air cleaner, dynamo and semi-circular fan housing are the most readily visible components, the cylinders being low down, hidden inside cooling air ducts.

Below: beetle-shaped bodywork earned the car its nickname in many languages and became familar almost all over the world. Considerations of structural rigidity and low wind resistance originally dictated the shape.

# 1957 Mercedes 300 SL

Rivals in their early pioneer years, the two great German firms Daimler (Mercedes) and Benz joined forces in 1926 and Mercedes-Benz vehicles established over the succeeding years an enviable reputation for sound engineering and high quality. Of the many impressive Mercedes-Benz production cars, none has been more dramatic or attracted a greater mystique than the 'gull wing' 300 SL. Its origins lie in motor racing. When Mercedes returned to competition in the early fifties, they began with sports car racing, running 300 SL coupés in prototype trim. They quickly proved more than a match for the opposing Aston-Martins, Jaguars, Ferraris, and others, finishing first and second in the 1952 Le Mans 24 hour race. Two years later, while the racing team had moved on to even faster machinery, including a highly successful Grand Prix car, a production version of the 300 SL appeared. Features of its design derived from the racing prototypes included a space frame chassis constructed of small diameter steel tube (a technique never before and rarely since used for road cars) and an engine fitted with fuel injection in place of carburetors. It was a bold, uncompromising concept. It was also expensive to make, and production continued for only three years. Mercedes have never marketed a true successor to the 300 SL.

Above: hot air from the engine compartment escapes through side vents to the rear of the front wheel arches. Functionalism in dramatic mood sets the style for the body design.

## Specification

**Engine:** Six cylinders, in line. Bore 85mm (3.3in), stroke 88mm (3.5in), displacement 2996cc (183cu in). Single overhead camshaft. Fuel injection. Coil ignition. Power output 215bhp.

**Transmission:** Four-speed gearbox, propeller shaft, rear swinging half-axles.

**Brakes:** Hydraulically operated drum brakes on all four wheels.

**Suspension:** Front, independent, coil springs and wishbones. Rear, independent, coil springs and swing axles.

**Wheelbase:** 2400mm (7ft 10.5in).

**Maximum speed:** 135mph (217km/h).

**Body:** Two-seater fixed-head coupé with 'gull wing' doors.

Above: prominent in the air intake opening at the front of the car is the three-pointed star of the Mercedes-Benz emblem.

Above: 1957 Mercedes-Benz 300 SL 'gull wing' coupé. The most exciting Mercedes car yet to be put into series production, this model is now recognised as a classic and has become something of a cult object among its devotees. Wheels have brake cooling slots and are secured with single central knock-off nuts, echoing racing practice. The body styling too maintains close links with the prestigious factory team sports racers such as the 300 SLR in which Stirling Moss and Denis Jenkinson gained a famous victory in the 1955 Mille Miglia race, averaging 100mph (160km/h) over 1000 miles (1600km) of ordinary Italian roads. Mechanically, the production car is a very long way from the eight-cylinder racing version. But it is impressive and powerful nevertheless, perhaps the most advanced sports car design of the fifties, translating research into practicality with very little compromise.

Right: multi-tube space frame chassis construction derived from racing car design necessitates high and wide body sills for structural rigidity. To lessen the difficulties of access to the cockpit which the sills create, the door openings extend into the roof, and this is the reason for the upward-swinging 'gull wing' doors which form the single most distinctive feature of the 300 SL in fixed-head coupé form.

Something in the Italian temperament responds to motoring in a way not quite paralleled anywhere else, and the history of the motor car in Italy is a passionate and sometimes dramatic one. Time and again, Italian cars manifest, on top of original, sound engineering, a certain extra flair, an expression of enthusiasm and zest, which puts them in a class of their own. The presence, in northern Italy, of a tradition of skilled craftsmanship allied to an almost infallible sense of good design, has made the country the home of both the best body builders and designers (Bertone, Giugiaro, Pininfarina, Zagato) and of a group of superb specialist car makers like Alfa Romeo (a 1929 1750 Super Sport model is shown here), Ferrari, Maserati, and Lamborghini.

# 1928 Lancia Lambda

Firmly placed among those manufacturers whose products have always been strongly marked with an individual character, whose designers have shown an original, creative flair, is the Lancia company. The first Lancia appeared in 1907, but the model which really established the reputation of the marque, Vincenzo Lancia's masterpiece, was the Lambda, introduced in 1923. In three areas, the Lambda was a radical departure from contemporary norms. The ingenious narrow angle engine, with all four cylinders, though in vee formation, contained in a single block and topped by a single cylinder head, left a large proportion of the chassis length free for passenger accommodation. While every other car maker almost without exception employed a rigid beam front axle, Lancia designed a system of coil sprung independent front suspension. While almost every other car had a chassis frame to which a separate body was attached, the lower body panels of the Lambda themselves formed the chassis in an integrated unitary structure. Independent suspension, integral construction, and attempts to achieve a compact power unit are the common currency of car design today: the Lambda was a brilliant precursor of things to come. And it proved to be a very satisfactory motor car, much liked.

## Vincenzo Lancia

Founder of the company, architect of the Lambda, and the driving force behind all the firm's designs up to and including the Aprilia of 1937, Vincenzo Lancia was a colourful figure and a powerful personality. Born in 1881, the son of a wealthy food manufacturer, he was apprenticed to the Ceirano car factory. When Fiat took the firm over he became chief inspector, and progressed to driving the works team racing cars. He competed with great gusto and some notable success in major events such as the Gordon Bennett races and the Targa Florio in the years up to 1907. In 1906 he formed his own company, and subsequently proved himself a capable, original and inventive car designer. He never raced his own cars, though they achieved distinction in competition in other hands. The badge adopted by Lancia in 1911 was designed by another great enthusiast for the automobile, Count Carlo Biscaretti di Ruffia.

## Specification

**Engine:** Four cylinders in narrow V. Bore 82.55mm (3.25in), stroke 120mm (4.7in), displacement 2570cc (157cu in). Shaft driven overhead camshaft. Magneto ignition. Power output 69bhp at 3500rpm.

**Transmission:** Four-speed gearbox, propeller shaft, live axle.

**Brakes:** Mechanically operated drum brakes on all four wheels.

**Suspension:** Front, independent, coil springs and sliding pillars. Rear, semi-elliptic leaf springs.

**Wheelbase:** 3100mm (10ft 2in).

**Maximum speed:** 75mph (120km/h).

**Body:** Four-seater Torpedo tourer.

**Above: compact narrow angle V4 Lancia engine has a single overhead camshaft under a deep, curved top cover.**

Above: 1928 Lancia Lambda eighth series tourer. The standard Lambda bodywork was classically simple, being changed only in detail through the model's seven year production run.

Left: one of the Lambda's most advanced features was the sliding pillar independent front suspension. Unconventional at this period, when the beam axle was almost universal, it continued to be used on Lancia cars right up to the sixties.

Below: driving position of the Lambda. The dashboard is well stocked with dials right across its width.

# 1933 Alfa Romeo 8c 2300

The marque Alfa Romeo, one of the most celebrated in the history of sports and racing cars, derives its name from those of Nicola Romeo, engineer and entrepreneur, and the ALFA company (Anonima Lombarda Fabbrica Automobili, which translates roughly as Lombard Cars Inc) which he took over in 1915. ALFA had been founded in 1909 by Cavaliere Ugo Stella, who had begun, like a number of other European car makers, by building French designed Darracqs under licence. Based in Milan, Alfa Romeo continued to use the ALFA badge composed of two of the early heraldic emblems of that city, the cross and the serpent. With a series of sports and racing machines built in the twenties and thirties, the company established a reputation as makers of excellent thoroughbred motor cars, a reputation it has retained in post-war years in spite of moving towards larger volume production. Taut, balanced, and responsive, the cars of Alfa Romeo epitomize the pulse-quickening appeal of the sports car at its best.

## Jano's engine

At the heart of the Alfa Romeo 2300 is the superb engine designed by Vittorio Jano, who joined Alfa from Fiat in 1923 at the instigation of Enzo Ferrari, then working for Alfa and subsequently, of course, famous for his own cars. Jano created for Alfa a virtuoso series of interrelated engine types, each one beautifully engineered and remarkably efficient, which put the company in the forefront of sports and racing car builders. First came the eight-cylinder P2 Grand Prix car. Then followed the six-cylinder 1500 and 1750 sports cars, and, in 1931, the eight-cylinder 2300. The light alloy crankcase of this unit carries the crankshaft in no less than ten main bearings. The crankshaft is in two halves, bolted together at the centre where the gears to drive the twin overhead camshafts and auxiliaries are fitted. The gear train, which also drives the supercharger, runs between two identical alloy cylinder blocks, each containing four linered bores. The cylinder head, likewise, is in two identical halves, with inclined valves and hemispherical combustion chambers. In its original standard form this engine produced 130 to 135bhp at 4900rpm.

**Left: rear view of a 1933 Alfa Romeo 8c 2300 long chassis sports car. The finned tail panel conceals the spare wheel and there is a tonneau cover over the rear seat area. Four-seater bodywork was required by the regulations of the Le Mans 24 hour sports car endurance race, which was won by Alfas of this type every year from 1931 to 1934. This particular example was taken to second place in the 1935 race by French drivers Dreyfus (who used the pseudonym 'Heldé' and Stoffel.**

Below: by 1933 the sports car was no longer so unremittingly stark and angular as it had been, as the battery box-cum-step faired into the rear fender of the Alfa shows. The filler pipe is for the centrally mounted oil reservoir tank of the dry sump engine lubrication system.

Above: classic lines of the pre-war Alfa sports car. In this view, the appearance is similar to the more numerous six-cylinder 1750 type. Less than 200 of these eight-cylinder 2300 models were built. Large brake drums, finned to improve cooling, are the external evidence of the car's racing background. The magnificent twin overhead camshaft engine under the hood is a close relative of the units used in two of Alfa's successful Grand Prix cars, first the Monza version of 1931 to 1933, and then the 1932 P3, the first ever single seater (or Monoposto'), a milestone in design and one of the most famous of all racing machines.

**Specification**

**Engine:** Eight cylinders, in line, in two blocks of four. Bore 65mm (2.6in), stroke 88mm (3.5in), displacement 2336cc (143cu in). Two gear driven overhead camshafts. Roots type supercharger. Coil ignition. Power output 142bhp at 5000rpm.

**Transmission:** Four-speed gearbox, propeller shaft, live axle.

**Brakes:** Mechanically operated drum brakes on all four wheels.

**Suspension:** Semi-elliptic leaf springs front and rear.

**Wheelbase:** 3100mm (10ft 2in)

**Maximum speed:** 102mph (165km/h).

**Body:** Two/four-seater sports.

# 1934 Lancia Augusta

Outwardly, there is little to distinguish this 1934 Augusta from other typical small or medium size sedans of the period, except perhaps that it is more stylish than many. But closer examination reveals that it is a true Lancia under the skin, directly descended from the Lambda which established the strain. The sliding pillar front suspension is there. The engine, though the smallest Lancia had yet made, is another narrow angle V4. And the Augusta represents a return to unitary construction, the last of the Lambdas and the intervening models (Dilambda, Astura, and Artena) having reverted to separate chassis so that specialist coachbuilders could create limited production styles. New ground was broken by the Augusta, the first Lancia to have hydraulic brakes. After the Augusta came the Aprilia, the last of Vincenzo Lancia's personal designs, launched in 1937, the year of his death. But Lancia cars went on: the distinctive front suspension was in use until 1963, and the last of the narrow vee engines was used in the Fulvia from 1963 to 1972. In recent years, Lancia's absorption into the Fiat empire has completed the circle begun when the founder left Fiat seventy years earlier. Some rationalization has resulted, but enthusiasm survives unabated.

Left: traditional radiator grille and badge identify this stylish little sedan as a Lancia. Better roadholding than the average domestic equivalent earned Lancias something of a sporting reputation, echoed in the wire wheels and knock-off hub caps of this example.

## Specification

**Engine:** Four cylinders in narrow V. Bore 69.9mm (2.75in), stroke 78mm (3.0in), displacement 1196cc (73cu in). Chain driven overhead camshaft. Coil ignition. Power output 35bhp at 4000rpm.

**Transmission:** Four-speed gearbox, propeller shaft, live axle.

**Brakes:** Hydraulically operated drum brakes on all four wheels.

**Suspension:** Front, independent, coil springs and sliding pillars. Rear, semi-elliptic leaf springs.

**Wheelbase:** 2650mm (8ft 8in).

**Maximum speed:** 63mph (102km/h).

**Body:** Four-door sedan, unitary structure.

Above: with the Augusta, Lancia added to their range a smaller and cheaper model than they had marketed before, and it was manufactured and sold in larger numbers than any previous car they had made. Unitary construction facilitated volume production. A distinctive feature of many four-door Lancia models is the way in which front and rear doors are hinged at opposite ends, and shut together at the centre with no fixed pillar between them. This 'pillarless' style, evidence of the designers' confidence in the rigidity of the basic structure, is seen on the Augusta, had been used on some earlier Dilambda and Artena models, and was to be employed later on the Aprilia, Ardea, Aurelia, and Appia. All these models manifested in one way or another the distinctive Lancia flair for cars of quality and character.

# 1935 Fiat tipo 508S Balilla

In 1899 a group of forward-looking businessmen in Turin formed a company to embark on the manufacture of that exciting new arrival on the scene, the motor car. The company was soon well known by its initials, FIAT (Fabbrica Italiana Automobili Torino). Under its able chairman Giovanni Agnelli, grandfather of the present head, the new firm quickly prospered and grew. Today, Fiat is an industrial giant whose activities embrace civil engineering as well as the manufacture of buses, other commercial road vehicles, railway trains, marine engines, aircraft and aero engines, machine tools, and much else besides, But cars remain at the core: Fiat put Italy on wheels, unrivalled in the home market, as well as becoming a major exporter. In another country, this role as the mass supplier of transportation might have bred only cars of stolid utility, dependable but dull. But in Italy, somehow, the motor car has never been purely utilitarian: from its makers, its mechanics, and many of its drivers it evokes a special kind of irrepressible enthusiasm. This is reflected time and again in those subtleties of design, hard to pin down, that combine to distinguish what can only be called a driver's car from mere transport. So clearly present in the products of the smaller, more specialised manufacturers (Alfa Romeo, Ferrari, Lancia), this quality has regularly bubbled up at Fiat too, as this delightful little tipo 508S Balilla sports of 1935 bears witness.

## Specification

**Engine:** Four cylinders, in line. Bore 65 mm (2.6 in) stroke 75 mm (3.0 in), displacement 995 cc (61 cu in). Pushrod operated overhead valves. Coil ignition. Power output 36 bhp at 4400 rpm.

**Transmission:** Four-speed gearbox, propeller shaft, live axle.

**Brakes:** Hydraulic footbrake on all four wheels. Handbrake on transmission.

**Suspension:** Semi-elliptic leaf springs front and rear.

**Wheelbase:** 2300 mm (7 ft 6.5 in).

**Maximum speed:** 70 mph (113 km/h).

**Body:** Two-seater sports.

## Balilla history

The Balilla began as an inexpensive family car, launched in 1932. Features distinguishing it from broadly similar bread-and-butter offerings from other firms were a high top gear, efficient hydraulic brakes, and an engine which, though still a side valve layout, was of shorter piston stroke, thus potentially smoother and more durable, than its rivals. A sports-bodied version which appeared in 1933 achieved some success in the Mille Miglia road race.

But the big step forward came in 1934 with a new overhead valve cylinder head, boosting power output by fifty per cent. The result was a capable little sports car much praised for its handling, braking, and high cruising speed.

**Left: A distinctive feature is the prominent fin on the cover over the rear compartment which houses the spare wheel. Cars for the British market, such as this one, were imported in chassis form and had bodies fitted in Britain.**

**Top: Italian sporting style. Long, flared front wings and a raked radiator grille create a flowing line. Contemporary MG and Singer sports models from Britain, by contrast, were much more square cut and upright.**

**Above: Simple, round dials grace the functional dashboard layout with rev counter and speedometer predominating. Spring spoked steering wheel and fold flat windshield were fashionable wear for sports cars of the period.**

# 6 SPAIN

Today, Spain plays a significant part in the multi-national European motor industry, with factories affiliated to several of the major groups. The Seat company builds local variants of Fiat designs, Fasa is a Renault subsidiary, and there is a former Chrysler factory now under the Peugeot umbrella. The construction of a new plant near Valencia formed an important part of the planning of Ford's Fiesta project. In the past, firms like Nacional Pescara and Pegaso built sports cars. But apart from all this, one marque alone, Hispano-Suiza, would guarantee Spain an entry in any motoring anthology, as the imperious 1928 model shown here demonstrates. Hispano, too, was a multi-national enterprise, with a Swiss designer and a factory in France as well as Spain.

# 1912 Hispano-Suiza 'Alfonso'

In the early days of motor racing there were, in addition to the races run for cars of virtually unlimited engine size, events for smaller machines, 'voiturettes', restricted at first by a weight limit and later by engine size regulations. For four or five years up to 1910, this category was dominated by French cars, Sizaire-Naudins and Lion-Peugeots with grotesquely long-stroke single and twin cylinder engines. King Alfonso XIII of Spain, an ardent motoring enthusiast, persuaded Hispano-Suiza, the only Spanish car manufacturer at the time, to contest this French supremacy. Hispano designer Marc Birkigt prepared a team of four cylinder voiturettes in 1909. Success was not immediate, but for the Coupe de l'Auto race at Boulogne in 1910 the Hispanos had been developed to a point where they completely outclassed the single and twin cylinder opposition and ushered in a new era of more sophisticated racing machines. From this successful 2.6 litre racer, Birkigt developed a 3.6 litre road car. The sporting qualities of this model pleased the King, who owned several and made long and fast journeys at the wheel, and it soon became known as the Alfonso XIII. Though of much smaller engine capacity than almost all the other contemporary cars with sporting pretensions, the Alfonso was able to compete on equal terms with most of them.

## Birkigt and Hispano-Suiza

Marc Birkigt, Hispano-Suiza designer from 1904 to 1934, was born in Geneva, Switzerland in 1878. An able student of engineering and physics, his first concern was with electric traction, and it was this which took him to Barcelona to work on a funicular railway and a battery-powered bus project. While there he became involved with the design of early cars for La Cuadre and Castro. The financial difficulties of the latter firm led to the formation of Hispano-Suiza. Birkigt designed a range of large and luxurious cars, which first brought the company to the king's notice, and then the Alfonso model. The overhead camshaft V8 aero engine he designed — licence-built by firms in several countries — powered a large proportion of allied aircraft during the First World War. The stork blazon, carried by French ace Guynemer on his SPAD fighter, evolved into a mascot carried on the radiator cap of many of the superb Hispanos in the twenties. Like all the truly great car designers, Birkigt brought to his work a combination of artistry and technical skill.

## Specification

**Engine:** Four cylinders, in line. Bore 80mm (3.2in), stroke 180mm (7.0in), displacement 3620cc (221cu in). Side valves, T head. HT magneto ignition. Power output over 60bhp.

**Transmission:** Multi-disc clutch, three-speed gearbox, propeller shaft, live axle.

**Brakes:** Foot-brake on transmission, hand-brake on rear wheels.

**Suspension:** Semi-elliptic leaf springs front and rear.

**Wheelbase:** 2642mm (8ft 8in).

**Maximum speed:** 70mph (112km/h).

**Body:** Two/three-seater sports.

Above: looking light and poised, almost spidery yet not frail, the 1912 Hispano-Suiza conveys an impressive sense of the 'rightness' of its design to the observer. Well balanced for good handling, not unnecessarily heavy, and powered by a simple and effective (if somewhat dated) engine, the Alfonso model was an outstanding automobile in its day and is often cited as one of the first true sports cars.

Far left: winged Hispano-Suiza badge carries Spanish and Swiss emblems. The name commemorates the company's Spanish origin and the Swiss nationality of its designer, Marc Birkigt. Hispanos were built in Barcelona, Spain, and also, later, at a factory in France.

Left: Birkigt's four-cylinder engine has a single cylinder block with integral head. Valves are arranged on each side of the block in a T head layout, inlet valves on the right, exhaust valves on the left. A removable screw cap is fitted above each valve position, those on the inlet side carrying compression or priming taps. The carburetor is bolted straight onto the engine, feeding into inlet tracts incorporated in the block casting. This engine develops its maximum power at 2300rpm, an usually high speed for its period.

# Best Loved Cars of the World

**Acknowledgements**
The publishers would like to thank the National Motor Museum at Beaulieu, Hampshire, England, for their kind permission to reproduce all of the illustrations in this book.